THE CULTURAL POLITICS OF 'POSTMODERNISM'

Edited by
JOHN TAGG

ISBN 0-9621899-0-1

Current Debates in Art History is distributed by

MRTS
State University of New York
Binghamton, NY 13901
607-777-6758

Cover: Victor Burgin's "Office at Night."
photograph courtesy of John Weber Gallery, New York City.

THE CULTURAL POLITICS OF 'POSTMODERNISM'

Edited by
JOHN TAGG

Current Debates in Art History, One
Managing Editor: George McKee

Department of Art and Art History
State University of New York at Binghamton
1989

Notes On Contributors

Victor Burgin is Professor of Art History at the University of California at Santa Cruz. He is the author of *Work and Commentary, The End of Art Theory*, and *Between*, and the editor of *Thinking Photography* and *Formations of Fantasy.*

Barbara Correll is an Assistant Professor of English at the University of Tulsa.

Hal Foster is a freelance critic, teaching modern critical theory at the Pratt Institute and the New School for Social Research. He is the author of *Recodings: Art, Spectacle and Cultural Politics* and the editor of *The Anti-Aesthetic: Essays on Postmodern Culture, Discussions in Contemporary Culture*, and *Zone.*

Frederick Garber is Professor and Chair, Department of Comparative Literature, SUNY Binghamton, and author of *The Anatomy of the Self from Richardson to Huysmans.*

Stephen Melville is Associate Professor of English at Syracuse University and author of *Philosophy beside Itself.*

Constance Penley is Associate Professor of English and Film Studies at the University of Rochester and an editor of the journal *Camera Obscura.*

Stephen David Ross is Professor and Chair of the Philosophy Department, SUNY Binghamton. His recent books include: *Perspective on Whitehead's Metaphysics; A Theory of Art: Inexhaustability by Contrast*, and *Learning and Discovery: the University and the Development of the Mind.*

John Tagg is Associate Chair of Art and Art History at SUNY Binghamton, author of *The Burden of Representation: Essays on Photographies and Histories* and editor of Max Raphael's *Proudhon, Marx, Picasso.*

Maureen Turim is Associate Professor in the departments of Cinema and Comparative Literature, SUNY Binghamton, and the author of *Abstraction in Avant-Garde Films.*

Michael Walsh is Assistant Professor of English at the University of Connecticut at Hartford.

Contents

Acknowledgements

"THE CULTURAL POLITICS OF 'POSTMODERNISM'" WAS THE FIRST ANNUAL SYMposium on *Current Debates in Art History*, organized by John Tagg, and held on 25 April 1987 in the Department of Art and Art History of the State University of New York at Binghamton. Subsequent to the symposium, "Geometry and Abjection" appeared in *Cultural Analysis, Psychoanalysis and Cultural Theory*, edited by James Donald and published by Macmillan, London; and "Time Travel, Primal Scene and the Critical Dystopia" was published in *Camera Obscura*, number 15, Summer 1987. Michael Walsh's review of the conference appeared in *C. E. P. A. Quarterly*, Spring/Summer 1987, volume 2, Issue 3/4. "Postmodernism and the Born-Again Avant-Garde" was first published in *Block*, number 11, Winter 1985/6.

We are grateful for permission to publish these articles here.

Current Debates in Art History 1

Preface

THE CULTURAL POLITICS OF "POSTMODERNISM" IS A PARTIAL RECORD OF THE PROceedings of the first in a new series of annual symposia which, over the years to come, will set out not only to explore, but also to intervene within as wide a range as possible of "Current Debates in Art History." At the mention of "Art History," it might be expected that I shall go on to make the now customary derogatory remarks about the discipline. Over the past twenty years, it has become almost a convention that debates in Art History should be opened with laments or apologies for the wretchedness of the subject: for its backwardness, for its institutional insularity and intellectual isolation, for its standing as the last bastion of reactionary thought in the academy, and so on. But we begin with no such apologies.

Certainly, comfortable definitions of the area, its objects of study and patterns of explanation, have been shaken in Europe and North America of late, as much by the consequences of an unprecedented expansion of higher education and leisure consumption, as by the impact of new kinds of theory, new kinds of interest, and new kinds of art historian drawn from groups which had had no previous stake in the discipline or the traditions it sought to construct. But, in this, Art History's troubles have been much the same as those of other traditional departments of the "humanities"—and deservedly so. Yet, with a generation of academics risen from the counter courses of the Sixties to varying degrees of comfort and prominence in departments whose names they still dispute, and with doctoral theses being prepared on the histories of the radical journals in which we wrote our denunciations and critiques, it is clear that the old simplifications will no longer do. Notions of the supposed unity and motivation of a "dominant" or even a "bourgeois" Art History look as dubious now as the attempts they shored up in the Seventies to foreclose debate around a supposedly coherent and oppositional "Social History of Art."

I say this with no satisfaction and certainly not to be reconciled with the discipline, nor to reinstate an unhappy pluralism or deadly decorum of no debate. It seems to me that the argument needs to be sharpened not relaxed. Nor do I believe for one moment that we are all liberals or postmoderns now. But the grounds of our differences, the discursive and institutional spaces for struggle, and our unchosen and perhaps unflattering positions within them, have become much harder to articulate. The goals, too, have become harder to define or justify without the guarantees of historicism, humanism, or ideology critique. This loss can precipitate us into post-structuralist depression, or it can make the need for an agreement to argue even more urgent and underline the purpose of this series, outside the safe-house of polemical position conferences, and without the convenience of exaggerated justificatory images of a shabbily regressive discipline or a resurrected Art History strategically placed—as film theory once allegedly was—to synthesize cultural and political theories and analyses.

There are some, no doubt, who would want to argue that the complexity and theoretical diversity I point to in Art History are no more than ideological symptoms of a larger process which can be known: expressions of the momentum of Late Capitalist incorporation, remorseless commodification and "postmodern" proliferation. The problems here are ones taken up in the symposium itself and they bring me, rhetorically if not logically, to the theme of this collection: *The Cultural Politics of "Postmodernism"*—chosen precisely because it marks a particularly visible point of eruption of unfamiliar theoretical discourses within the domain of Art History, and because this eruption gives Art History a place in the debate, while simultaneously opening its concerns beyond their narrow academic limits. (Thus, the contributors are rightly and pointedly inter- or even un-disciplinary.) Yet, paradoxically, *The Cultural Politics of "Postmodernism"*—written that way to register a break or hesitation—also perhaps marks within this wider debate the return of the repressed: a certain familiar mode of art critical and art historical thinking that, since Roger Fry, has been very partial to the prefix "post" and the suffix "ism" and to the historical and theoretical unities they claim to block in. For all the voraciousness of the term, that makes a conference *on* "postmodernism" soon became a conference *in* postmodernism, it had to be put at the outset that we might need to worry somewhat about this word and look quizzically at the conditions and consequences of what, at least from an English perspective, is the extraordinary consolidation of the term in American cultural theory, for all the divergences of its currencies.

The papers gathered here respond to this question in very different ways. The aim was not to present the appearance of a coherent overview, but to initiate a debate. It is all the more regrettable, therefore, that practical and financial considerations prevented the inclusion of discussion from the floor and exchanges between speakers. The papers, however, are largely unrevised; though, in place of an introduction, I have included an earlier essay of my own which provides some clues to the thinking behind the organization of the symposium.

I want to thank all those who participated in or attended the conference, especially Mary Law and Philip Armstrong for their organizational support, and William Spanos, whose contribution could not be included. Subsequently, it has been the hard work of George McKee, Nancy Hamme, and the staff of MRTS, and the financial support of the State University of New York at Binghamton, that has made it possible to present the debate in published form.

John Tagg

Papers

Introduction: Postmodernism and the Born-Again Avant-Garde

JOHN TAGG

MY POINT OF DEPARTURE IS ONE OF THE MOST TENACIOUS NARRATIVES OF CONtemporary art history and theory. Easy target for more than a decade, it seems now that news of its death has been greatly exaggerated. With variously motivated attempts to salvage something from the centerless art practices of the late seventies and early eighties, debate has turned again on the concept of modernism, seen now in relation to what is increasingly called postmodernism. The term has been invoked in a confusing variety of contexts and has a number of conflicting currencies. I do not want, however, to spend much time on its cruder apologists. There are of course those who, adapting the prescriptions of Clement Greenberg, have tried to prolong what he divined as the project of a fleeting American avant-garde by means of an even severer selectivity. To avoid having to notice the loss of an earlier modernism's ethical and political mission and the presence of more embarrassing things, their critical gaze has fixed on the fetishism of formal innovation, whose subtleties define monolithic periods and movements named according to their place in a linear or cyclical temporality, in which they are always before something and after something else: Impressionism or Post-Impressionism, early Cubism or late, painterly abstraction or postpainterly abstraction, modernism or postmodernism. Against the advocates of such stoic disavowal stand the more knowing celebrants of novelty, for whom the renewal of art is more readily equatable with the renewal of the market for art. They cheerfully admit to the waning of heroic rhetoric and the decline of the high moral tone but welcome hectic diversity and the penetration of the art world by the values and practices of consumer production, as more fitting to the mood and structure of postindustrial and postmodern society. Some go further and see eclecticism and self-referential play (now made respectable under the borrowed name of intertextuality) as representing a new content and direction—"The New Spirit in Painting" giving unified expression to a "Zeitgeist" in which all the old beliefs and antagonisms are outmoded, and talent and technology are all. Poor old Hegel. He's been back as tragedy and as farce and is down to a big prize TV game.

But I don't want to be delayed by this from turning my real attention to a body of analyses critical of this celebratory commercialism, whose various modes of address to the notion of postmodernism still appear to return us to the structures of a familiar cultural theory and historiography. I turn first to the French philosopher Jean-François Lyotard, whose writings from the past decade and a half are enjoying a new currency if not a vogue in Britain and the USA now. Lyotard rejects one form of capitalist postmodernism as commercial eclecticism—"the degree zero of contemporary general culture"—which evades the challenge of authentic research and in which the only criterion is profit.[1] Yet he welcomes the splintering of social life and the destructuring of individual experience, which he connects to a general crisis in representation in science and art. For Lyotard, ideas of a unified subject, the transparency of the sign to its referent, socio-cultural unity and a unitary end to history are dangerous fictions of Hegelian inspiration which can only be maintained by one sort of terror or another. Modern means of image transmission and information storage have vastly multiplied such realist fantasies of an organically unified society, transparent to itself, free from doubt, and evolving along a controlled and predictable line. Offered as visions of efficiency or liberation, such fantasies are always apologies for order, authority and control, pressed, at a time of crisis of all legitimations, with ever increasing violence. Whether made in the name of profit or the name of social policy, calls for unity, order, identity, security, unmediated communication and stabilized meanings come only from the voice of authoritarian conservatism and are always linked to the liquidation of experimental avant-gardes. The link is justified because avant-gardes, by questioning the rules of art, have called into doubt the very notions of "reality" and "identity" which dominate Party solutions and mass communications. Avant-garde artists know that modernity cannot exist without the shattering of every kind of belief and the invention of other realities. True postmodernism, Lyotard insists, is the challenging of all that has been received.

What is extraordinary, however, is that from the shards of this shattered whole, Lyotard retrieves his own unity. Postmodern thought and postmodern art have thrown aside the security blankets of belief, the consoling myths and legitimizing narratives of the past, and have called into question the adequacy of every discourse in order to present the sublime fact that the unpresentable exists. On this level, the analysis of postmodern aesthetics may be transferred to the concurrent crisis of scientific knowledge. There is a single line of questioning and a single compulsion: the urge to make new. Art interrogates itself to the end of intelligibility, challenging all forms of presentation in its drive to impart a sense of the unpresentable. Postmodern science, working without the consolation of truth or the legitimizing myth of human liberation, challenges all established statements and narratives as it continually generates more work and infuses the repressive system with new and unknown desires. The diversity of experimentation and dissent is gathered up in the unity of the mission of the avant-garde to challenge the very structures of meaning of society. Like John Wayne, out of the smoke and dust of the postmodernist explosion, we begin to see the familiar chunky outlines of a rough but redeeming modernism. There is the singleness of purpose, the showdown on the frontier of the possible, the fearless interrogation, the high-noon drama on which hangs the fate of social, psychological and epistemological renewal, the restless need for change, now stripped of any illusion of progress, but with its eyes fixed on a horizon which is endlessly different yet somehow always the same. If this is postmodern, it is evidently not a radical break with modernism but a moment of the same structure, opening on the production of ever new modernisms. As Lyotard insists:

> Postmodernism thus understood in not modernism at its end but in the nascent state, and this state is constant.[2]

The difficulty with this reassertion of the modernist idea that art has the crucial if feared ability to transform meaning and value for the surrounding society is that it assumes too much in the continuity of context and fails to explain the changing relation of avant-garde practices to capitalist production, dominant cultures and state apparatuses. How, in his rush to embrace every excessive act of postmodernity, can Lyotard avoid being caught in a compromising position with the eclectic cultural commodities he scorns? Artists like the New York video maker Martha Rosler have become well aware of the problem. Her work has been focused by a situation in which it has become difficult to distinguish between the turn-over of styles of the newly successful art and that of other commodities, especially those produced by an "entertainments industry" which "has become the prime source of cultural goods and self-images for a western world now well on its way to cultural hegemonisation."[3] Rosler also has less nostalgia for a cultural modernism which conservative critics may blame for the ungovernability of western societies, but which has also operated a mechanism of exclusion, marginalising black, gay, Third World and female artists, and securing a position of privilege for the exemplary white, European oriented, male. If there has recently been any wavering in this, it has only been to "supply the necessary transfusion of energy and style" to the system and to conjure away social conflict by a "symbolic acceptance of the socially dispossessed." The problem remains the high density of corporate culture and its endlessly adaptable capacity for incorporation. It has to be fought not by the tactics of the vanguard but by a post-Cuba style guerrilla war.

> It is only through a "guerrilla" strategy which resists a deadly universalization of meaning by retaining a position of marginality, that the production of critical meanings still remains possible. It is only on the margins that one can still call attention to what the "universal" system leaves out.[4]

It may be noticed that the struggle of marginals imagined here bears a distinct resemblance to Lyotard's formulation and, as with Lyotard, the idea belongs with a cluster of others whose persistence in Rosler's arguments returns her perilously close, in certain respects, to the theories she seeks to oppose. The unqualified antipathy to mass culture, for example, and the determination to open up a rift between it and authentic art has a history going back, through the influential arguments of *Partisan Review* in the 1940s, in which Greenberg's ideas were formed, to nineteenth century conservative cultural theory and evaluative aesthetics. It depends from a view of culture as the production of key values or the expression of significant human meanings allowing insight into society as a whole. It is also linked to a privileging of the Artist as maker of these meanings, as socially or spiritually empowered to adjudicate on abiding human values. This notion of the Artist as specially endowed persists in and, indeed, has been very much attached to the view of the artist as outsider, heroine on the margins, or guerrilla in the cultural ghetto. The idea is still that the future of significant culture lies in the hands of the embattled few.

This exclusive mission is, however, only an elitist or utopian fantasy. Marginality guarantees nothing. Culture is not expressive of an experience to be had on the margins or anywhere else; and, contrary to what is suggested, belligerent independence is not the artist's natural or necessary state. What is rather the case is that formations which represent themselves as heroically isolated—that is, avant-gardes—have only emerged under special historical conditions. Avant-gardism is not an inescapable artistic fate or a process inherent in the history of art. It is a social strategy by which artists both engage with and differentiate themselves from the contemporary field of cultural politics. The role, function and representation this strategy gives to artists belong to a particular historical pattern which has been important only in certain conjunctures—Paris in the 1850s and 1870s, for example, or New York in the 1940s. Such avant-gardes, however, were never outside the social order in the ways they represented themselves as being. Indeed, the form of their dislocation both from the dominant national culture and from any popular base cannot be understood outside the particular cultural, political and economic conditions which made it possible. Avant-gardism and modernist ideals developed only within certain metropolitan intellectual formations at particular stages in the history of not yet stabilized capitalist states. These formations depended on metropolitan centers for their arenas of intervention, for their institutional bases, for their access to publicity and communications, and for the professional and leisure class audiences which could support their activities. Their particular conditions of existence cannot, therefore, be generalized as giving access to an enduring predicament of artists, culture, or humanity. Moreover, the meaning and value of the avant-garde stance changed with changing conditions. A strategy which opened up certain sets of possibilities in one moment was overtaken by the growth of corporate monopolies, by the restructuring of the relations of capital and the state, by the remobilisation of nationalism, by the break up of traditional cultural formations, and by processes of professionalisation, suburbanisation, and redeployment, all of which affected cultural activities in First World countries in the postwar period. Such processes transformed avant-garde formations in complex ways and gave them new meanings. But the transformations cannot be adequately described by the hold-all term postmodernism; just as they cannot be understood as a simple process of incorporation, and they cannot be challenged by yet tighter definitions of outsiderness or newer forms of avant-gardism. The point about American Abstract Expressionism, for example, is that it constituted the appropriation and reassertion of a European cultural practice at a time in the USA when the relations of artists, art institutions, corporate structures and the state had changed. The point is not that it expressed the aspirations of corporate capitalism or that the artists who practiced it were either unwitting dupes of some grand conspiracy or discredited hacks who sold out, who stopped being avant-garde enough. What's wrong is the avant-gardist analysis and the stance itself. What is needed is an alternative way of understanding culture and cultural conflict, very different from the one inherent in avant-gardism.

Perhaps, this is the moment to turn to Fredric Jameson whose recent, lengthy meditation on the subject argues, as I have done, that the unrealisable utopianism of modernist movements emerged in a definite socio-economic context.[5] From this, Jameson goes on to draw the conclusion that significant modifications in the role and dynamic of cultural practice must always be matched to the emergence of new social and economic relations. Just as the dominance of the realist mode was bound up with the formation of market capitalism, and the arrival of modernism with the development of monopoly and imperialism, so the eclipse of the authoritarian, moralist stance of high modernism and the waning of its monumental emotional import has been coincident with the spread of industrialization not only to all sectors of the economy but also to the sphere of circulation and the domain of culture. Postmodernism is therefore an historical not an aesthetic category, which constitutes not a stylistic option but the cultural dominant of late capitalism.

For Jameson, postmodernism may offer a strategy for surviving and producing new desires within the structural limits of capitalism, but it is not a revolution. He rejects the idea of the continuous, self-propelling generation of newness. Perpetual change must be seen as the rhythm of the capitalist mode of production itself and exhilaration with this rhythm as the reward and lure by which the social reproduction of capitalism is accomplished. In this sense, postmodernist innovation is a function of the late capitalist system, not a subversion of it, and the fundamentally anarchist approach to science and art it fosters is simply unable to confront the challenge of an international cultural commodity market and a global monopoly of information systems. Such monopolies, like the rest of the private property system, cannot be expected to be transformed from within, but can be challenged "only by a genuinely political (and not symbolic or protopolitical) action."[6]

It is a telling point against those taken with the idea of a "guerrilla rhetoric." But let us pause to consider the theoretical structure—and especially the concept of culture and the place of the political—which generates such an analysis. What seems to underlie Jameson's virtuoso polemic and his notion of dominant cultural norms is a return to something like the Lukacsian notion of culture as the reflex or expression of an homogeneous structure whose character and history are ultimately determined by economic processes.[7] From the point of view of the total structure, he sees late capitalism as expressing itself in the fragmentation and heterogeneity of postmodern cultural production. From the perspective of the particular cultural product, by an equation of function and meaning, he comes to a view of the work of postmodernist art as an expression of its newly developed function within a system of cultural commodities. The price of historicising and setting a limit to the cultural seems to have been the obliteration of its specificity and effectivity.

Beyond its wealth of reference, the extreme abstraction of Jameson's underlying analysis and the ultimate obscurity of the strategy he proposes for an acceptable practice, which will somehow express the global system, correspond to the level of generalization at which he sets the problem: how to posit a connection between culture in general and the socio-economic structure as a whole. Yet, we can reject this level of abstraction without falling back, as he thinks we must, into a particularist atomism in which everything is just different from everything else. Just as we can reject both Jameson's concept of the structure of the social and his analysis of meaning without being committed to an historical relativism of random and repressive difference, either as an apologist for consumer society or as an advocate of an anarchic avant-gardism. From the point of view of structure, there are clearly ways of theorizing totalities and the temporalities of historical change which do not invoke the holism and evolutionism of what Althusser called the expressive model. This is what Marx argued out across the pages of the *Grundrisse* notebooks in which he broke with Hegel's teleological notion of the social complex as an essential identity giving expression to a particular stage of a process of concentration described by the unfolding contradictions of the simple, unique, internal principle: the Idea. What Marx arrived at instead was a theory of articulation or representation, on the basis of which the economic structure—and, by extension, the social totality, always at a definite stage of historical development—could be conceived as a complex, conflictual and interactive totality, "a rich totality of many determinations and relations," as he put it, in which the dominant moment was production.[8] The idea of an inner structure or essence was effectively displaced. Similarly, from the point of view of the theory of meaning, following semiotic analyses, one can think of cultural practices as having definite conditions of existence which they do not determine without imagining that these are what they express. Cultural meanings are neither the reflection or reflex of a referent in an anterior reality, nor the expression of a primal experience which may be abstracted from its articulation in discourse. They are rather produced by determinate practices and their social consequences are always heterogeneous and open to dispute. Certainly, their production, circulation and consumption take place under given, though changeable, conditions in which their effects may be more or less constrained. But they are in no way the expression of these conditions.

How does this theoretical dispute about the nature of the social totality and the production of cultural meanings turn on the problems of modernism and postmodernism we have been looking at? Perhaps the first stumbling block is the idea of modernity itself. This is what proponents of modernism and postmodernism presuppose: a unity of experience prior to discourse and corresponding to a set of identifiable conditions; a global response to the global processes of socio-economic modernization; a continually renewed experience which issues somehow in an ever renewing series of expressions whose formal innovations testify to their modernness of content. The mechanism by which all this takes place is never certain but, given the panoramic reaches of space and time across which it must act, it can never be anything but grand and absolute. The "signs in the street" must all signify the same thing: the global signified—modernity.[9]

The problems of this theory lie both on the plane of synchronic relations and along the axis of historical change it implies. In the first place, that modernity which is affirmed in modernism is not a unified state of affairs evenly imposed in a uniformly postindustrial world. In the second place, as I insisted earlier, historical transformations—including the development of modernism—do not take place by a continuous replacement of one moment by another in a sequential series which is endlessly different but always the same. Both spatially and temporally, historical change is not even and continuous but complex and differential and internally heterogeneous. The rhythms of development and dispersal of industrial capitalism were neither smooth nor uninterrupted, and it was never evenly distributed across the globe. As Perry Anderson has argued, its irregular expansion and geographical unevenness give rise to a complex temporality woven of different and discontinuous strands.[10] The pattern is one of high complexity in which diverse and internally divided societies engage with industrialization under very different climatic, historical, political, and cultural conditions, and with very different relationships to the emergence of an increasingly international system of capital. The idea of a general and definable modernity is in retreat and with it the idea of a universalized modernism which is its alleged expression. Cultural production must necessarily exhibit a real, integral diversity which universalizing and homogenizing theories can only obliterate.

Even if we narrow our focus to those cultural groupings which were self-consciously modernist, we shall see only a diversity of formations and practices with different relations to capitalist development, national traditions, residual and dominant cultures and emergent social forces, and therefore with different meanings and effects. What is structurally similar in the confluences of conditions which determined the sporadic emergence of such modernisms cannot be assayed without first grasping this historical particularity. Only then will we be in a position to gauge whether certain combinations of factors were necessary to the existence of modernist and postmodernist formations and practices, whether and how these conditions and practices changed, how they interacted, and under what conditions they tended to disintegrate. Even then we must not make the mistake of seeing the various modernisms as reflections or expressions either of their conditions of existence or of some experience which these conditions allegedly determine. Modernist discourses are not simply media through which inner and socially determined experiences find outward expression and thereby recognition in the answering experience of others. The materiality of discursive practices, the impossibility of referring them back to some primal anterior reality, and the impossibility of abstracting experience from the discursive structures which articulate it, disrupt any simple notion of the determination of discourses by a sociality of which they are, in any case, a part.[11] The cultural value of modernisms cannot, therefore, be established by however patient a reconstruction of their social conditions. They can be evaluated only by tracing their structures and effects under changing circumstances in the societies in which they emerged, and by interrogating the relationship of these effects to their conditions of production and reception, their means of representation, and the practices through which these means were set to work. There can be no general answer to the question of the value of modernism. We cannot circumvent the task of historical analysis of the national cultural complexes and systems of international exchange across which modernisms claimed to have constructed a transcendent culture.

What then of the hopes for a radical, interventionist culture which the theories of modernism and avant-gardism seemed to hold out? We must be specific again. Such hopes have a history. It only makes sense to talk of cultural intervention and struggle in relation to societies which have developed certain forms of the state and elaborated a range of cultural institutions, and in which governmentality rests, at least in part, on the action of these institutions in securing the social relations which constitute the functioning social order. Cultural products and practices have significance precisely because of their place in that non-unitary complex of social practices and systems of representation which construct, invoke, maintain, or subvert the relations of domination and subordination in which social position and identity are produced. Such practices and representations must therefore affect, and be in turn affected by, political and economic conditions and conflicts, though they cannot be seen as their expression. Nor can they be evaluated be reference back to their origins or sources. Their only measure is the calculation of their specific social consequences— which is not to say that they determine their own conditions of existence or that these don't have effects. Cultural practices always involve the mobilization of determinate means and relations of representation within an institutional framework whose organization takes a particular historical form—marked in the West today, no doubt, by what Stuart Davis called "cultural monopoly."[12] There is no meaning outside this framework but it is not monolithic. The institutions which compose it offer multiple points of entry and spaces for contestation—and not just on the margins. The nature of the resistance will depend on the nature of the site. But the spaces are never isolated. Their relations and hierarchies also constitute specific levels of intervention, demanding their own specific forms of struggle.

It must be clear, therefore, that the variety and complexity of these spaces and hierarchies mean that no one strategy can be adequate to all confrontations. Lyotard is right to insist that we cannot repair the fragmentary character of culture and should not try. We are free of the burden of masterpieces. In Terry Atkinson's words: you can't have socialism in one work of art. But an equally pressing conclusion is that no one kind of person can do the job. The specialness of the artist, point of honour of the avant-garde and held fast even by practitioners like Rosler, can no longer serve even as a mobilizing myth. Cultural institutions require a whole range of functionaries and technicians who contribute their skills or service cultural production in a whole range of ways. A painting is as much a collective work as a film and only takes on the currency of social meaning through the application of multiple levels of expertise. It follows, then, that any adequate cultural intervention must be collective—as collective as advertising, television or architecture—as collective as the accumulated skills, the layers of habit, the practices and codes, production values, rituals of procedure, technical rules of thumb, professionalised knowledges, distinctions of rank, and so on, which make up the institutional base.

Success in such a strategy will be a matter for continual calculation and not a moral question settled once and for all at the imaginary threshold between incorporation and independence. It will be measured partially and locally, in the absence of generalized rules, from an always questionable internal perspective, caught in the totalizing system, seeking to link up with other localized eruptions of dissent, but without the security of the great narratives of legitimation which bolstered belief in change in the past. In this, Lyotard is right. But we shall also have to do without that story first told as a vision of utopian progress at the dawn of industrialization by followers of Saint Simon: I mean the fable of the avant-garde.[13]

Notes

1. Jean François Lyotard, "Answering the Question: What is Postmodernism?" in *The Postmodern Condition: A Report on Knowledge* (Minneapolis: University of Minnesota Press, 1984) 76.
2. Lyotard 79.
3. Martha Rosler, "Notes for a televised discussion of 'Art After Modernism'," *Voices*, April 11, 1984.
4. Ibid.
5. Fredric Jameson, "Postmodernism, or The Cultural Logic of Late Capitalism," *New Left Review* 146 (July–August 1984): 53- 92.
6. Fredric Jameson, "Foreword" to Lyotard, *The Postmodern Condition*, xxi.
7. In "Postmodernism, or The Cultural Logic of Late Capitalism," p. 57, Jameson argues that "postmodern culture is the internal and superstructural expression of a whole new wave of American military and economic domination throughout the world."
8. Karl Marx, *Grundrisse*, trans. Martin Nicolaus (Harmondsworth: Penguin, 1973) 100.
9. Cf. Marshall Berman, "The Signs in the Street: A Response to Perry Anderson," *New Left Review* 144 (March–April 1984): 114–23.

10. Perry Anderson, "Modernity and Revolution," *New Left Review* 144 (March–April 1984): 96–113.

11. Cf. Gareth Stedman Jones, *Languages of Class. Studies in English Working Class History 1832–1982* (Cambridge: Cambridge University Press, 1983) 20–22.

12. Stuart Davis, "Abstract Painting Today," in Francis V. O'Connor (Ed.), *Art For The Millions* (Greenwich: New York Graphic Society, 1973) 122.

13. Cf. Nicos Hadjinicolaou, "Sur L'Idéologie de L'Avant-Gardisme," *Histoire et Critique des Arts* 6 (July 1978): 49–76.

Geometry and Abjection

VICTOR BURGIN

Simple geometrical opposition becomes tinged with aggressivity

—Bachelard, *The Poetics of Space*

ALTHOUGH IT MAKES NO DIRECT REFERENCE TO ALTHUSSER'S 1970 PAPER, "Ideology and Ideological State Apparatuses,"[1] Roland Barthes' 1973 essay, "Diderot, Brecht, Eisenstein," has the effect of *spatialising* the Althusserian concept of ideology as *representation:* "there will still be representation for so long as a subject (author, reader, spectator or voyeur) casts his gaze towards a horizon on which he cuts out the base of a triangle, his eye (or his mind) forming the apex."[2] Laura Mulvey's 1975 paper, "Visual Pleasure and Narrative Cinema,"[3] subsequently theorised the voyeuristic subject of Barthes' theatrical space in terms of Freudian psychoanalysis. The change across this five-year period is profound. From a contingent set of ideas held in the mind—ideas which may be dissipated through exposure to reason—"ideology" now became conceived of in terms of a space of representations which the subject *inhabits*, a space to which there is neither outside nor end; a space, moreover, which the *desiring* subject negotiates through transactions which are predominantly *unconscious*.

For all the innovation, however, there remained significant ties with tradition. Barthes' optical triangle is, after all, one-half of the diagram of the *camera obscura*—a metaphor not unfamiliar to students of Marx. Further, 1975 was also the year of publication, in French, of Foucault's

Discipline and Punish.[4] Barthes' "eye at the apex" therefore easily became conflated with that of the jailor, actual or virtual, in the tower at the center of the Panopticon prison. For all that Foucault himself would have opposed it, this further contributed to the survival of that strand of theory of ideology according to which ideology is an instrument of domination *wielded* by one section of a society and *imposed* upon another—"the dominant ideas are the ideas of those who dominate." In this context, then—and given the urgent exigencies of a feminist *realpolitik*—it is not so surprising that one effect of Laura Mulvey's essay was to lead to an impasse in respect of man-made images of women, all of which, without discrimination, henceforth came to be viewed as instruments of sadistic objectification, and therefore as proscribed objects.

I believe that the metaphor of the "cone of vision," predominant in theories of representation over the past twelve years, is itself responsible for a reductive and simplistic equation of looking with objectification. In so far as this metaphor is drawn from physiological optics, it is inappropriate to the description of psychological functioning. In so far as it is drawn from Euclidean geometry, it is insufficient to that changed apprehension of space which is an attribute of our so called "postmodern" culture.

I

Space has a history. In the cosmology of classical Greece, as F. M. Cornford writes, "the universe of being was finite and spherical, with no endless stretch of emptiness beyond. Space had the form of . . . a sphere with center and circumference."[5] It is this classical space which, essentially, survived the Biblically derived "flat earth" of early Christian doctrine, to re-emerge in the late Middle Ages, where, by the thirteenth century, the world-view of Greek antiquity was to be restored. In medieval cosmology, supercelestial and celestial spheres enfolded a terrestrial space they did not touch—the scene of human action. In this space, every being, and each thing, had a place preordained by God, and under His omnivoyant gaze. Foucault has termed this medieval space, the "space of emplacement;" it is this space, he observes, that was effectively destroyed by Galileo:

> For the real scandal of Galileo's work lay not so much in his discovery, or rediscovery, that the earth revolved around the sun, but

> in his constitution of an infinite, and infinitely open space. In such a space the place of the Middle Ages turned out to be dissolved . . . starting with Galileo and the seventeenth century, extension was substituted for localisation.[6]

The vehicle of this changed cosmology was Euclidean geometry. Euclid's *Elements of Geometry* was written around 300BC. Husserl, in *The Origin of Geometry*, supposes that the system of Euclidean geometry arose out of practical activity, such as building. In the classical world, however, the space of the prevailing "common sense" cosmology seems to have been based upon visual observation rather than technique—the horizon appears to encircle us, and the heavens appear, to the eye, as vaulted above us. In the Renaissance, it is this conflict between observation and intellection, between hyperbolic and Euclidean spaces, which is played out in the early stages of the invention of perspective. That there is no necessary connection between knowledge of Euclidean geometry and the development of perspective is clear from the example of the Moslem world. In the West, the *primacy* of geometry over perception had been stressed in the Platonism of St. Augustine, who writes: ". . . reason advanced to the province of the eyes. . . . It found . . . that nothing which the eyes beheld, could in any way be compared with what the mind discerned. These distinct and separate realities it also reduced to a branch of learning, and called it geometry."[7]

Although dependent upon Euclid's *Elements of Geometry*, perspective in the Renaissance took its most fundamental concept from another work by Euclid, the *Optics*. The concept, of course, is that of the "cone of vision." It is this same cone which, some two thousand years after Euclid, Brunelleschi conceives of as intersected by a plane surface—the picture plane. By means of this model, something of the premodern worldview passes into the Copernican universe—a universe which is no longer geocentric, but which is nevertheless homocentric and egocentric. A basic principle of Euclidean geometry is that space extends infinitely in three dimensions. The effect of monocular perspective, however, is to maintain that this space *does* nevertheless have a center—the observer. By degrees, the sovereign gaze is transferred from God to "Man." With what Foucault calls the "emplacement" of the Medieval world now dissolved, this ocular subject of perspective, and mercantile capitalism, is free to pursue its entrepreneurial ambitions wherever trade winds blow.

Entrepreneurial humanism first took liberties with, then eventually replaced, theocentric determinism according to a model which is implicitly Aristotelian, and in a manner which exemplifies the way in which spatial concepts are projected into the representation of political relationships. In Aristotle's cosmological physics it was assumed that the preponderance of one or the other of the four elements first posited by Empedocles (earth, water, air and fire) would determine the natural place of that body within a continuum from the center to the periphery of the universe. This continuum of actual and potential "places" constituted space. Analogously, the idea that a human individual will find its natural resting place within the social space of differential privileges according to his or her inherent "qualities" has remained a cornerstone of humanist-derived political philosophies to this day. Newton disengaged space "as such" from Aristotelian "place,"[8] and Newtonian physics was in its turn overtaken by the physics of Einstein, in which, in the words of Minkowski: "space by itself, and time by itself, are doomed to fade away into mere shadows, and only a kind of union of the two will preserve an independent reality."[9] Most recently, the precepts of general relativity have themselves come into question in "quantum theory."[10] The cosmology of modern physics has nevertheless had little impact on the everyday world view in the West, which is still predominantly, an amalgam of Newton and Aristotelianism—"places in space," a system of centers of human affairs (homes, workplaces, cities) deployed within a uniformly regular and vaguely endless "space in itself."

In the modernist avant-garde in art, however, it is not unusual to encounter references to a mutation in the sense of space and time brought about by modern physics and mathematics. Thus, for example, in 1925, El Lissitsky writes: "Perspective bounded and enclosed space, but science has since brought about a fundamental revision. The rigidity of Euclidean space has been annihilated by Lobachevsky, Gauss, and Riemann."[11] It is nevertheless more common, with modernism, to find a changed apprehension of space ascribed not to concepts in science as such, but rather to *technology*. Thus, Vertov writes: ". . . I am the cinema-eye. I am a mechanical eye. I, a machine, can show you the world as only I can see it . . . I ascend with airplanes, I fall and rise together with falling and rising bodies."[12] Constrained by mechanical metaphors, Russian futurism, like cubism, the art practice which most dramatically marks the modernist break with previous representational forms, ultimately fails, notwithstanding El Lissitsky's pronouncement, to leave Euclid behind. The mirror of perspectival representation is broken only in order that its fragments, each representing a distinct point of view, be reassembled according to classical geometric principles— to be returned, finally, to the frame and the proscenium arch.[13]

With the Modern period, human space became, predominantly, space *traversed* (it is by this token that we judge that the prisoner has little of it). In the "postmodern" period, the speed with which space is traversed is, in effect, no longer governed by the mechanical speed of machines such as airplanes, but rather by the electronic speed of machines such as computers and video links, which operate at close to the speed of light. A mutation in technology therefore has, arguably, brought the technolo*gism* inherited from the spatial perceptions of Modernist aesthetics into line with the perceptions of modern physics. Thus, for example, Paul Virilio writes, "technological space . . . is not a geographical space, but a space of time."[14] In this space-time of electronic communications, operating at the speed of light, we see things, he observes, "in a different light"—the "light of speed."[15] Moreover, this space seems to be moving, once again, towards self-enclosure. For example, David Bolter, a classics professor writing about computer programming, concludes: "in sum, electronic space has the feel of ancient geometric space."[16] One of the phenomenological effects of the public applications of new electronic technologies is to cause space to be apprehended as "folding back" upon itself. Spaces which were once conceived of as separated, segregated, now overlap: live pictures from *Voyager II,* as it passes through the rings of Saturn, may appear on TV sandwiched between equally "live" pictures of internal organs, transmitted by surgical probes, and footage from Soweto. A counterpart in the political sphere of the fold-over spaces of information technologies is terrorism. In the economic sphere it is the global tendency of multinational capitalism to produce first world irruptions in third world countries, while creating second world pockets in the developed nations. To contemplate such phenomena is no longer to inhabit an imaginary space ordered by the subject-object "stand-off" of Euclidean perspective. The analogies which fit best are now to be found in non-Euclidean geometries—the topologist's Möbius strip, for example, where the apparently opposing sides prove to be formed from a single, continuous, surface.

Space, then, is not, as Kant would have it, the product of *a priori,* inherently Euclidean, categories of mind. It has a history, it is a product of representations. Premodern space is bounded, things within it are assigned a determinate place along a predominantly vertical axis—heaven-earth-hell," or the "chain of being," extending from God down to stones. Modern space (inaugurated in the Renaissance) is Euclidean, horizontal, infinitely extensible, and therefore in principle boundless. In the early modern period this is the space of the humanist subject in its mercantile entrepreneurial incarnation. In the late modern period it is the space of industrial capitalism, of the airplane and the assembly line, the space of an exponentially increased pace of dispersal, displacement, dissemination, of people and things. The "postmodern" space, the space of financial capitalism, is now this former space in the process of imploding, infolding; to appropriate a Derridean term, it is a space in process of "intravagination." Guy Debord spoke of the first intimations of this, twenty years ago. He wrote of the unified space of capitalist production, "which is no longer bounded by external societies," the abstract space of the market, which "had to destroy the autonomy and quality of places," and he commented: "this society which eliminates geographical distance reproduces distance internally as spectacular separation."[17] Such "internal distance" is that of *psychical space*. Nevertheless, as I have already remarked, psychoanalytically inspired theories of representations over recent years have tended to remain faithful to the Euclidean geometrical-optical metaphors of the modern period.

II

At the very summit of her 1975 exposition of Lacan's concept of "The Imaginary,"[18] Jacqueline Rose places a quotation from Lacan's first seminar (1953–54): "I cannot urge you too strongly to meditate on the science of optics . . . peculiar in that it attempts by means of instruments to produce that strange phenomenon known as images."[19] As already observed, 1975 was also the year of publication of Laura Mulvey's "Visual Pleasure and Narrative Cinema" with its own emphasis on, in Mulvey's words, "the voyeuristic-scopophilic look that is a crucial part of traditional filmic pleasure." If we re-read these two papers today then we should read them in tandem, as the one is an essential, albeit somewhat contradictory, complement to the other.

In terms of theories of visual representations (in Britain and the US) Laura Mulvey's essay is, arguably, the single most influential article of the 1970s, and it is worth reminding ourselves of the context in which it first appeared.[20] It is now a commonplace to observe that there is a fundamental difference between "classic" semiology, which reached its apogee in the mid–1960s, and semiotics since about 1970. It is a difference, which in principal affects not only semiotics, but any theoretical practice whatsoever. It is this: the classical subject-object dichotomy is now "deconstructed." Today, we can no longer leave the interpreter outside of the act of interpretation. Today, the subject is part of the object.

As I have already remarked, in theories of representation the image of the "cone of vision," inherited from classical perspective, was used to make this insight clear to us. If the theme of "the look," then seems to dominate anglophone theories of film and photography during the 1970s (entering theories of painting in the 1980s), it is perhaps because, apart from the urgent sexual-political questions it could access, the accompanying image of the cone of vision simultaneously functioned as an *aide-mémoire* for a fundamentally important epistemological break in Western intellectual history.

In the 1970s, the cone of vision, model was often found conjoined with Lacan's concept of the "mirror-stage." Thus in Laura Mulvey's essay, for example, Lacan's early geometric perspective version of the Imaginary provides a model of cinematic "identification" in opposition to identification's own "mirror image"—scopophilic objectification. However, as Jacqueline Rose's article on the Imaginary is at pains to point out,

> it is precisely at the moment when those drives most relevant to the cinematic experience as such start to take precedence in the Lacanian schema [she refers to the scopic and invocatory drives] that the notion of an imaginary plenitude, or of an identification with a demand sufficient to its object, begins to be undermined.[21]

On the one hand, the model of the cone of vision was serving, valuably, to reinstate the previously ideologically elided presence of the observer in the space of representation. On the other hand, it was complicit in preserving what was most central to the ideology it sought to subvert—that punctual ego which Lacan identifies, in his later extended critique of the geometric perspective model of vision, as assuming that it can "see itself seeing itself." That much of the point of the Lacanian critique of vision had been lost is nowhere better indicated than in the debates which followed Mulvey's influential paper, which so often revolved around the objection that Mulvey had said nothing about the position of the *women* in the audience.

We see here precisely what Rose identifies as the "confusion at the basis of an 'ego psychology,' " which is, "to emphasize the relationship of the ego to *the perception-consciousness system* over and against its role as fabricator and fabrication, designed to preserve the subject's precarious pleasure from an impossible and non-compliant real"[22] (my emphasis). This confusion is supported and compounded by the cone of vision model of representation. Certainly, as already noted, the model teaches us that the subject is an intrinsic part of the system of representation, in so far as the image projects its lines of sight to an ideal point where that subject is supposed to be; nevertheless, the object here is quite clearly maintained as external to the subject, existing on the same plane in a relation of "outside" to the subject's "inside." The object of psychoanalysis, the lost object, may thus easily become confused with some real object. As Rose indicates, it is precisely for this reason that Lacan subsequently abandons the geometric perspective model.

"The idea of another locality," writes Freud, in a famous phrase. "The idea of another space," adds Lacan, "another scene, the *between perception and consciousness*"[23] (my emphasis). Psychoanalysis reveals unconscious wishes, and the fantasies they engender, to be as immutable a force in our lives as any material circumstance. They do not however belong to material reality but to what Freud termed "psychical reality." The space where they "take place"—"between perception and consciousness"—is not a material space. In so far, therefore, as Freud speaks of "psychical reality," we are perhaps justified in speaking of "psychical space." In the passage I have already quoted, Barthes speaks of representation as taking place whenever the subject "cuts out the base of a triangle, his eye (or his mind) forming the apex." "His eye or his mind . . ."—here, clearly, psychical space is conflated with the space of visual perception, which in turn is modelled on Euclid. But why should we suppose that the condensations and displacements of desire show any more regard for Euclid's geometry than they do for Aristotle's logic? Some of the peculiar spatial properties of the theatre of desire are indicated by Freud in his paper, "A Child is Being Beaten."[24] Here, the subject is positioned in the audience, *and* on the stage—where it is both aggressor and aggressed. The spatial qualities of the psychical *mise-en scène* are clearly non-Euclidean: different objects may occupy the same space at the same (non)instant, as in condensation in dreams; or subject and object may collapse one into the other. As Rose observes, what this paper most fundamentally reveals is "the splitting of subjectivity in the process of being held to a sexual representation (male or female)."[25]

"Author, reader, spectator or voyeur," writes Barthes, identifying his subject of representation. All of these subjects desire, but none more *visibly* than the voyeur. In the chapter of *Being and Nothingness* which bears the title, "The Look," and to which Lacan refers in his own extended discussion of the look as conceived in terms of geometric perspective, Sartre chooses to speak of his "being-as-object for the Other" from the position of the voyeur: "Here I am bent over the keyhole; suddenly I hear a footstep. I shudder as a wave of shame sweeps over me. Somebody has seen me. I straighten up. My eyes run over the deserted corridor. It was a false alarm. I breathe a sigh of relief." But, Sartre continues, if he now persists in his voyeuristic enterprise,

> I shall feel my heart beat fast, and I shall detect the slightest noise, the slightest creaking of the stairs. Far from disappearing with my first alarm, the Other is present everywhere, below me, above me, in the neighboring rooms, and I continue to feel profoundly my being-for-others.[26]

As Lacan puts it, "I am a picture" (just as I was God's picture in the medieval space of emplacement).

If Sartre had been less hostile to the concept of the unconscious he might not have excluded his condition of "being-for-others" from his relation to the object of his scopophilic interest. Merleau-Ponty's phenomenolgy moved towards a rapprochement with psychoanalysis (in a preface he contributed to a 1960 book on the work of Freud he spoke of a "consonance" between the two disciplines). Chapter IV of Merleau-Ponty's final, unfinished work, *The Visible and the Invisible*, is titled, "The Intertwining—The Chiasm." (*Chiasm*, an anatomical term for the crossing over of two physiological structures, is derived from a Greek root which means, "to mark with a cross." We make a cross by placing one line "across" another, but when we look at this figure we may *see* two distinct right-angled figures—each the reflection of its inverse other, and which only barely touch each other. Appropriately, then, the same Greek root has also given us the term *Chiasmus*—the rhetorical term for the trope of "mirroring.") The emphasis upon the *alienation* of subject and object, which is so often found in readings of Lacan's 1936 paper on the mirror-stage,[27] is absent from this essay from a man whose work so impressed Lacan (an essay in which we discover the "chiasm" in "chiasmus"). Merleau-Ponty writes:

> since the seer is caught up in what he sees, it is still himself he sees: there is a fundamental narcissism of all vision. And thus, for the same reason, the vision he exercises, he also undergoes from the things, such that, as many painters have said, I feel myself looked at by the things, my activity is equally passivity—which is the second and more profound sense of the narcissism: not to see in the outside, as the others see it, the contour of a body one inhabits, but especially to be seen by the outside, to exist within it, to emigrate into it, to be seduced, captivated, alienated by the

> phantom, so that the seer and the visible reciprocate one another and we no longer know which sees and which is seen.[28]

Fenichel begins his 1935 paper "The Scoptophilic Instinct and Identification" by remarking on the ubiquity of references to the incorporative aspects of looking—for example, in folk tales in which "the eye plays a double part. It is not only actively sadistic (the person gazing puts a spell on his victim) but also passively receptive (the person who looks is fascinated by that which he sees)."[29] He adds to this observation a reference to a book by G. Roheim on "looking-glass magic;" the mirror, Fenichel observes, by confronting the individual with their own ego in external bodily form, obliterates "the dividing-line between ego and non-ego." We should remember that Lacan's paper on the mirror-stage concerns a *dialectic* between alienation and identification, an identification not only with the self, but also, by extension, with other beings of whom the reflected image is a simulacrum—as in the early phenomenon of transitivism. Fenichel observes:

> one looks at an object in order to *share in* its experience. . . . Anyone who desires to witness the sexual activities of a man and woman really always desires to share their experience by a process of empathy, generally in a homosexual sense, i.e. *by empathy in the experience of the partner of the opposite sex*[30] [my emphasis].

As I have already observed, as far as is known, it never occurred to Euclid to intersect his cone of vision with a plane surface. This idea, giving birth to perspective, is attributed to the fifteenth century architect Filippo Brunelleschi, who gave a famous practical demonstration of his invention. Using his perspective system, Brunelleschi painted a picture of a church upon a panel. In order that the viewer see the image from the correct position—the true apex of the cone of vision—Brunelleschi made a small hole in the panel. The viewer, from a position behind the panel, looked through the hole into a mirror. What the viewer then saw was not him or herself, nor the reversed image of the screen behind which he or she was concealed. What they saw was the church of Santo Giovanni de Firenze, and the Piazza del Duomo. A contemporary observer wrote:

> he had made a hole in the panel on which there was this painting . . . which hole was as small as a lentil on the side of the painting, and on the back it opened out pyramidally, like a woman's straw hat, to the size of a ducat or a little more. And he wished the eve to be placed at the back, where it was large, by whoever had it to

> see . . . it seemed as if the real thing was seen: and I have had it in my hand, and I can give testimony.[31]

To my knowledge, and surprise, Lacan never spoke of Brunelleschi's experiment. But this hole in the panel, "like a woman's straw hat," is the same hole through which Norman Bates peers in Hitchcock's *Psycho.* We could have saved Janet Leigh if we had been able, there and then, to arrest this eye in the name of a moral certainty. In reality, there would have been no other choice. We should not, however, confuse police work with psychoanalysis, nor with art criticism, nor with art. It is a mistake to take observable behavior for psychical truth. The cone of vision model, however, encourages precisely this misrecognition. As Sarah Kofman writes in her book on the model of the camera obscura, "All these specular metaphors imply the same postulate: the existence of an originary sense . . . the "real" and the "true" pre-exist our knowledge of them."[32]

The model of the cone of vision, as it functions in 1970s theory, has a positive and a negative aspect. On the positive side, it reinstates the elided place of the subject in the space of representation; on the negative side, it maintains a subject-object dichotomy as a relation of inside/outside, underwriting that familiar confusion in which the psychical becomes a mere supplementary appendage to the space of the social. It is thanks to such positivism, for example, that certain critics can pay lip service to psychoanalytic theory while speaking of scopophilia as if there were nothing more to say about it than that it is a morally reprehensible form of behavior of men.

Catherine Clément has described Lacan's "era of models" as falling into two distinct periods. The first is a time of points, lines, arrows and symbols—a time of two-dimensional representations. The second period, "began when he realised that two dimensions were not enough to make his audience understand the theory of the unconscious as he conceived of it: specifically, he wanted to show that the unconscious is a structure with neither an outside nor an inside."[33] To this second period belong the topological models—the torus, the Möbius strip, the Klein bottle—objects which, "gave him the means to represent forms without insides or outsides, forms without boundaries or simple separations, forms of which a hole is a constitutive part."[34] Clément concludes that such geometrical models "merely complicated the exposition of his ideas." However, in the special case of the application of psychoanalytic theory to questions of "visual" art, I believe this metamorphosis of models provides a necessary corrective to a too-easy confluence of psychoanalytic concepts with some familiar prejudices of positivist- intuitionist art theory and criticism—a discourse always too ready to collapse sexuality into gender, psychology into sociology, too ready to take for granted precisely that sexual *difference* which psychoanalysis puts in question.

III

No space of representation without a subject, and no subject without a space it is not. No subject, therefore, without a boundary. This, of course, is precisely the import of the mirror stage: the founding Gestalt, the matrix within which the ego will take place. For Kristeva, however, there is a necessary gesture anterior to this first formation of an uncertain frontier in the mirror stage, a prior demarcation of space, in so far as geometry is a science of boundaries; and in a certain reading of Kristeva, we might say that the origin of geometry is in *abjection*.[35]

As a concept, the "abject" might fall into the gap between "subject" and "object." The abject, however, is in the history of the subject, prior to this dichotomy. The abject is the means by which the subject is first impelled towards the possibility of constituting itself as such—in an act of revulsion, of expulsion of that which can no longer be contained. It is significant that the first object of abjection is the pre-Oedipal mother—prefiguring, at the level of the individual, that positioning of the woman in society which Kristeva locates, in the patriarchal scheme, as perpetually at the boundary, the borderline, the edge, the "outer limit"—that place where order shades into chaos, light into darkness. It is this peripheral ambivalence of the position allocated to woman, says Kristeva, which has led to that familiar division of the field of representations in which women are either saintly or demonic—according to whether they are viewed as bringing the darkness, or keeping it out. Certainly, in Kristeva's work, the "feminine"—in the wider sense she has given this term—is seen as marginalised by the symbolic, patriarchal, order, but it is biological *woman* herself that this order abjects, in the form, specifically, of the procreative body. In *The Revolution of Poetic Language*, Kristeva writes,

> It is not the "woman" in general who is refused all symbolic activity and all social representativity. . . . That which is . . . under the sign of interdiction is the reproductive woman, through whom

> the species does not stop at the "imaginative producer" and his mother, but continues beyond, according to a natural and social law.[36]

The woman's body, that is to say, reminds men of their own mortality. When Narcissus looks into this abjected pool, of milk and blood, he sees the pale form at the feet of Holbein's ambassadors. Thus, in *Powers of Horror*, Kristeva reiterates, "Fear of the archaic mother proves essentially to be a fear of her generative power. It is this power, dreaded, that patrilineal filiation is charged with subduing."[37] Thus, in the rites with which certain tribal peoples surround menstruation, Kristeva identifies a fear of what she calls the *"power of pollution."*[38]

There is an extraordinary passage in Plotinus[39] in which this particular apparition of the abject is allowed to reveal itself in a discourse created precisely to conceal it. Plotinus has been speaking of beauty, he continues:

> But let us leave the arts and consider those works produced by Nature and admitted to be naturally beautiful which the creations of art are charged with imitating, all reasoning life and unreasoning things alike, but especially the consummate among them, where the moulder and maker has subdued the material and given the form he desired. Now what is the beauty here? *It has nothing to do with the blood or the menstrual process:* either there is also a color and form apart from all this or there is nothing unless sheer ugliness or (at best) a bare recipient, as it were the mere Matter of beauty [my emphasis].

And he asks:

> Whence shone forth the beauty of Helen, battle-sought; or of all those women like in loveliness to Aphrodite; or of Aphrodite herself; or of any human being that has been perfect in beauty; or of any of these gods manifest to sight, or unseen but carrying what would be beauty if we saw?[40]

Plotinus' platonic answer to his own question is, of course, the "Idea." What is abjected here—distanced by that figure of *accumulation*, that wave of perfect beings which carries the speaker away—is the body itself, as the mere matter of beauty. The abjected matter of which Kristeva speaks, from fingernail clippings to faeces—all that which we must shed, and from which we must distance ourselves, in order to *be*, in order, as we say, to "clear a space for ourselves." "It has nothing to do with . . .," writes Plotinus, in a figure close to that which classical rhetoric named *preterition*, but which must wait another fifteen hundred years for Freud to conceptualise as *negation*—for, of course, it has everything to do with Plotinus's desire. We have only to view the abject from a certain angle to see the form of category which might have been known to Plotinus, from a text of Longinus, "the sublime." Thus, in its eighteenth century incarnation, at the edge of Romanticism, in Shaftesbury: "the rude rocks, the mossy caverns, the irregular unwrought grottos and broken falls of waters, with all the horrid graces of the wilderness itself . . . these solitary places . . . beauties which strike a sort of melancholy."[41] For all the detailed discussion recently devoted to the sublime, I still see in this category a *simple* displacement, a banal metaphorical transference of affect from the woman's body to these caverns and chasms, falls and oceans, which inspire such fervent ambivalence, such a swooning of identity, in these Romantic men.

"Beauties which strike a sort of melancholy"—in *Soleil Noir* Julia Kristeva shows me the path which leads from beauty to an object I have lost, or which has abandoned me;[42] I also know that depression may be the mask which anger wears—the elegance of the concept of the sublime may be the sublimation of a more violent fear. Speaking in the voice of fascism he describes, here is Klaus Theweleit in *Männerphantasien:*

> If that stream reaches me, touches me, spills over me, then I will dissolve, sink, explode with nausea, disintegrate in fear, turn horrified into slime that will suffocate me, a pulp that will swallow me like quicksand. *I'll be in a state where everything is the same, inextricably mixed together*[43] [my emphasis].

It proves, finally, to be not woman *as such* who is abjected, but rather woman as privileged signifier of that which man both fears and desires: *the extinction of identity itself.* In the terms of the thermodynamic model which informs Freud's concept of the death drive, what is feared is the "entropy" at work at the heart of all organization, all differentiation. In religious terms, it is the indifferent "dust" to which we must all return. The transient matter of the woman's body however is doubly abjected, in that it is chronically organized to remind us, at monthly intervals, of our common condition as brief events in the life of the species. By this same token, however, the woman also signifies precisely that *desired* "state where everything is the same:" the pre-Oedipal bliss of that fusion of bodies in which infant and mother are "inextricably mixed together;" that absence of the *pain* of differing, condition of identity and meaning, whose extinction is deferred until death.

IV

Apropos of looking, Sartre writes, ". . . it appears that the world has a sort of drain hole in the middle of its being and that it is perpetually flowing off through this hole."[44] It is perhaps this same intimation of loss in the register of the visual which the Quattrocento defended itself against by fetishistically turning the intuition into a *system:* "perspective"—built not only upon a founding subject, the "point of view," but also upon the disappearance of *all things* in the "vanishing point." Previously, there had been no *sign* of absence—the *horror vacui* was a centerpiece of the Aristotelian system. In classical cosmologies, space is a plenum. Similarly, in the medieval world, God's creation is a fullness without gap. In Quattrocento perspective, the viewing subject first confronts an *absence* in the field of vision, but an absence disavowed: the vanishing-point is not an *integral* part of the space of representation; situated on the horizon, it is perpetually pushed ahead as the subject expands its own boundary. The *void* remains abjected. In later, non-Euclidean, geometry we find the spherical plenum of classical cosmologies collapsed upon itself to enfold a central void. For Lacan, this figure, that of the "torus," can represent a psychical space in which the subject repetitively comes into being, in a procession which circumscribes a central void—locus of the lost object and of the subject's death.

Much has been made of the insecurity of the "postmodern condition," and of its attendant "crisis of representation." There is nothing new in insecurity; it is the very condition of subjectivity, just as it is the condition of representation to be in crisis. This is not to say, however, that nothing changes. I have argued that our space has changed around us and that our former optical models for negotiating it are now out of their time. In "Women's Time," Kristeva has spoken of a mutation of space, a new "generation" of "corporeal and desiring mental space," in which "the very dichotomy man/woman as an opposition between two rival entities may be understood as belonging to metaphysics;" and she asks: "what can 'identity,' even 'sexual identity,' mean in a new theoretical and scientific space where the very notion of identity is challenged?"[45]

In this changed space, this new geometry, the abject can no longer be banished beyond some charmed, perfectly Euclidean, circle. The postmodern space of our "changing places" can now barely accommodate its old ghettos; they are going the way of the walled city-state. Perhaps we are again at a moment in history when we need to define the changing geometries of our changing places. I do not believe that it is a time when an art/theory which thinks of itself as "political" should admonish, or exhort, or proffer "solutions." I believe it is a time when it should simply *describe*. Perhaps it is again, at this time of post-industrial revolution, the moment for a realist project. It cannot, of course, be what it was at the time of Courbet, or even of Brecht. Attention to psychical reality calls for a *psychical realism*—impossible, but nevertheless. . . .

Notes

1. Louis Althusser, "Ideology and Ideological State Apparatuses (Notes Towards an Investigation)," in *Lenin and Philosophy and Other Essays* (London: New Left Books, 1971).

2. Roland Barthes, "Diderot, Brecht, Eisenstein," in *Image-Music-Text* (New York: Hill and Wang, 1977) 69.

3. Laura Mulvey, "Visual Pleasure and Narrative Cinema," *Screen*, vol. 16, no. 3 (Autumn, 1975): 6–18.

4. Michel Foucault, *Discipline and Punish* (London: Penguin, 1977).

5. Francis MacDonald Conford, *Plato's Cosmology* (New York: Harcourt, Brace, 1937).

6. Foucault, "Of Other Spaces," *Diacritics*, vol. 16, no. 1.

7. Augustine *De ordine* 15.42, in Albert Hofstadter and R. Kuhns (eds.) *Philosophies of Art and Beauty* (Chicago: University of Chicago Press, 1976) 180.

8. "Absolute space in its own nature, without relation to anything external, remains always similar and immovable. Relative space is some movable dimension or measure of the absolute spaces; which our senses determine by its position to bodies; and which is commonly taken for immovable space," Newton, *Mathematical Principles of Natural Philosophy*, quoted by Frank Durham and R. Purrington *Frame of the Universe* (New York: Columbia University Press, 1983) 156.

9. Minkowski, "Space and Time," in A. Sommerfeld (ed.) *The Principle of Relativity* (New York, 1923).

10. "For example, at extremely short distances, on the order of 10^{-33} cm, the geometry of space is subject to *quantum fluctuations*, and even the concepts of space and space-time have only approximate validity," Durham and Purrington, 191.

11. El Lissitsky, "K. und Pangeometrie," quoted in Pierre Descargues, *Perspective: History, Evolution, Techniques* (New York: Van Nostrand Reinhold, 1982) 9. It is necessary to distinguish between "Non-Euclidean geometry" (or *metageometry*) and "n-dimensional geometry" (or *hypergeometry*). The former, initiated in the nineteenth century by Gauss and Lobachevsky and developed by Riemann

is a geometry of curved surfaces – spaces which are boundless and yet finite; the latter, also developed in the nineteenth century, is the geometry of "hyperspace," a hypothetical space of more than three dimensions. The idea of a fourth dimension as a *literal* fact gained much popularity from the close of the nineteenth century and into the 1930s and exerted some considerable influence on the early modern movement in painting, not least in its more mystical formulations (the fourth dimension as "higher reality," for example, in the Theosophism of Kandinsky and Mondrian). Beyond the 1920s, however, after the popular dissemination of the ideas of Einstein and Minkowski, the idea of a fourth dimension of space largely gave way to the idea of a four-dimensional spatio-temporal continuum with *time* as the fourth dimension. See Linda D. Henderson, *The Fourth Dimension and Non-Euclidean Geometry in Modern Art* (Princeton: Princeton University Press, 1983).

12. D. Vertov, "Film Directors, A Revolution," *Lef*, vol. 3, in *Screen Reader* 1 (1977):286.

13. At this point, the necessary simplicity of my outline risks an injustice to Vertov. The industrial-materialist emphasis of some Russian Formalism was asserted against the mysticism which had entered early Russian Futurist art, primarily from the philosophy of P. D. Ouspensky. In *Tertium Organum* (1911), Ouspensky identifies the "fourth dimension" (see note 11, above) as that of the Kantian "noumena," and allocates to the artist the function of revealing that "higher" world "beyond" phenomena. When, in 1913, the Futurist Matyushin translated extracts from Gleizes and Metzinger's *Du Cubism* (1912) for the journal *Union of Youth*, he accompanied them with passages from *Tertium Organum*. In the same year, Mayakovsky published "The New Art and the Fourth Dimension" in which he counters the notion of a higher, non-material, reality with the assertion that the "fourth dimension" is simply that of *time:* "There is in every three- dimensional object the possibility of numberless positions in space. But to perceive this series of positions ad infinitum the artist can only conform to the various moments of time (for example, going around an object or setting it in motion)," quoted in C. Douglas, *Swans of Other Worlds: Kazimir Malevich and the Origins of Abstraction in Russia* (Ann Arbor, UMI Research Press, 1980) 31. Mayakovsky's observations adequately describe the program of French Cubism (which, in today's terms, we might say "shatters the object," rather than deconstructs the subject-object dichotomy); further, his observations are in agreement with Eisenstein's subsequent thought: "the fourth dimension (time added to the three dimensions)," "The Filmic Fourth Dimension" (1929) in J. Leyda, (ed.) *Film Form: Essays on Film Theory* (New York, 1949) 69. Vertov's "unmotivated camera mischief" (Eisenstein), on the other hand, often seems to point outside such accommodation of ideas from "n-dimensional geometry," and towards the "wrap-around" spaces of Non-Euclidean geometry (Information in this note derived from Henderson, *The Fourth Dimension*.)

14. Paul Virilio, *L'Espace Critique* (Paris: C. Bourgeois 1984).

15. Virilio, *Speed and Politics* (New York: Semiotext[e], 1986).

16. David Bolter, *Turing's Man: Western Culture in the Computer Age* (Chapel Hill: University of North Carolina Press, 1984).

17. Guy Debord, *Society of the Spectacle* (Detroit: Black & Red, 1983) paragraph 167.

18. Jacqueline Rose, "The Imaginary," in *Sexuality in the Field of Vision* (London: Verso, 1986).

19. Jacques Lacan, *La Séminaire, livre I: Les écrits techniques de Freud* (Paris: Seuil, 1975) 90.

20. We should also, incidentally, bear in mind that Mulvey herself has continually denounced the widespread attempt to freeze an evolving argument—an argument to be traced through her film-making, as well as through her writing—at that particular, 1975, frame.

21. Rose, 182.

22. Rose, 171.

23. Lacan, *The Four Fundamental Concepts of Psychoanalysis* (London: Hogarth, 1977) 56.

24. Sigmund Freud, " 'A Child is Being Beaten:' A Contribution to the Study of the Origin of Sexual Perversions," *The Standard Edition of the Complete Psychological Works of Sigmund Freud,* (London: Hogarth Press, 1953–74) 17:175–204.

25. Rose, 210.

26. Jean-Paul Sartre, *Being and Nothingness* (New York: Washington Square Press, 1966) 369–70.

27. Laura Mulvey's article is clear in its insistence on the Narcissistic, identificatory, aspect of looking (see section I, B). However, in this article, identification is seen uniquely as "that of the spectator fascinated with the image of his like,. . . and through him gaining control and possession of the woman within the diegesis;" Mulvey, 13.

28. Maurice Merleau-Ponty, *The Visible and the Invisible* (Evanston: Northwestern University Press, 1968) 139.

29. "The Scoptophilic Instinct and Identification," in H. Fenichel and D. Rapaport (eds.) *The Collected Papers of Otto Fenichel,* First Series (New York: Norton, 1953), 375.

30. Fenichel 377.

31. Antonio Manetti, *Vita di Filippo di Ser Brunellesco,* ed. Elana Tosca (Rome, 1927) 11ff. quoted by John White, *The Birth and Rebirth of Pictorial Space* (London: Faber, 1972) 116.

32. Sarah Kofman, *Camera Obscura de l'Idéologie* (Paris: Galilée, 1973).

33. Catharine Clément, *The Lives and Legends of Jacques Lacan* (New York: Columbia University Press, 1973) 160.

34. Clément, 161.

35. In a response to this paper (at a conference at the University of Warwick, May, 1987) Kristeva said she would "more cautiously" prefer the word "precondition," rather than "origin," here; she referred to abjection as the "degree zero of spatialisation," adding, "abjection is to geometry what intonation is to speech."

36. Julia Kristeva, *La révolution du langage poétique* (Paris: Seuil, 1974) 453.

37. Kristeva, *Pouvoirs de l'horreur* (Paris: Seuil, 1980) 92.

38. Kristeva, *Pouvoirs* 93.

39. My thanks to Francette Pacteau for having shown this passage to me.

40. Plotinus, *Ennead I,* Eighth Tractate, Beauty; quoted by A. Hofstadter and R. Kuhns, *Philosophies of Art and Beauty* (Chicago: University of Chicago Press, 1964) 152.

41. Shaftesbury, "The Moralists," Part III, Section II, in Hofstadter and Kuhns 245–46.
42. Kristeva, *Soleil Noir: Dépression et Mélancolie* (Paris: Gailímard, 1987) 107ff.
43. Klaus Theweleit, *Male Fantasies* (Oxford: Polity, 1987).
44. Sartre, 343.
45. Kristeva, "Women's Time," in T. Moi, (ed.) *The Kristeva Reader* (Oxford: Blackwell, 1986) 209.

Time Travel, Primal Scene, and the Critical Dystopia

CONSTANCE PENLEY

IF THE SURE SIGN OF POSTMODERN SUCCESS IS THE ABILITY TO INSPIRE SPIN-OFFS, *The Terminator* was a prodigy. The film was quickly replicated by *Exterminator, Re-animator, Eliminators, The Annihilators*, and the hardcore *The Sperminator*, all sound-alikes if not look- alikes. It then went on to garner one of popular culture's highest accolades when a West Coast band named itself *Terminators of Endearment*. And just to show that postmodernity knows no boundaries, national or otherwise, an oppressively large (2 ft. x 3 ft.) and trendy new Canadian journal has appeared, calling itself *The Manipulator*.

For some science fiction critics, Fredric Jameson among them, *The Terminator*'s popular appeal would represent no more than American science fiction's continuing affinity for the dystopian rather than the utopian, with fantasies of cyclical regression or totalitarian empires of the future. Our love affair with apocalypse and Armageddon, according to Jameson, results from the atrophy of utopian imagination, in other words, our cultural incapacity to imagine the future.[1] Or, as Stanislaw Lem puts it, in describing the banality and constriction of most American science fiction, "The task of the SF author today is as easy as that of the pornographer, and in the same way."[2] But surely there are dystopias and dystopias, and not all such films (from *Rollerball* to *The Terminator*) deserve to be dismissed as trashy infatuations with an equally trashy future. While it is true that most recent dystopian films are content to revel in the sheer awfulness of The Day After (the Mad Max trilogy and *A Boy and His Dog* come of readily to mind), there are others which try to point to present tendencies that seem likely to result in corporate totalitarianism, apocalypse, or both. Although *The Terminator* gives us one of the most horrifying post-apocalyptic visions of any recent film, it falls into the latter group because it locates the origins of future catastrophe in decisions about technology, warfare and social behavior that are being made today. For example, the new, powerful defense computer that in *The Terminator* is hooked into everything—missiles, the defense industry, weapons design—and trusted to make all decisions, is clearly a fictionalized version of the burgeoning Star Wars industry. This computer of the near future, 40 years hence, gets smart—a new order of intelligence. It "began to see all people as a threat," Reese tells Sarah as he tries to fill her in on the future, "not just the ones on the other side. It decided our fate in a microsecond. Extermination."

A film like *The Terminator* could be called a "critical dystopia" inasmuch as it tends to suggest causes rather than merely reveal symptoms. But before saying more about how this film works as a critical dystopia, two qualifications need to be made. First, like most recent science fictions from *V* to *Star Wars*, *The Terminator* limits itself to solutions that are either individualist or bound to a romanticized notion of guerilla-like small-group resistance. The true atrophy of the utopian imagination is this: we *can* imagine the future but we *cannot* conceive the kind of collective political strategies necessary to change or ensure that future. Second, the film's politics, so to speak, cannot be simply equated with those of the "author" James Cameron, the director of *The Terminator*, whose next job, after all, was writing *Rambo* (his disclaimers about Stallone's interference aside, he agreed to the project in the first place). Instead, *The Terminator* can best be seen in relation to a set of cultural and psychical conflicts, anxieties and fantasies that are all at work in this film in a particularly insistent way.

Tech Noir

What are the elements, then, of *The Terminator's* critical dystopian vision? Although the film is thought of as an exceptionally forward-thrusting action picture, it shares with other recent science fiction films, like *Blade Runner*, an emphasis on atmosphere or "milieu," but not, however, at the price of any flattening of narrative space. (In this respect it is closest to *Alien*.) *The Terminator* is studded with everyday life detail, all organized by an idea of "tech noir." Machines provide the texture and substance of this film: cars, trucks, motorcycles, radios, TVs, time clocks, phones, answering machines, beepers, hair dryers, Sony Walkmen, automated factory equipment. The defense network computer of the future which decided our fate in a microsecond had its humble origins here, in the rather more innocuous technology of the film's present. Today's machines are not, however, shown to be agents of destruction because they are themselves evil, but because they can break down, or because they can be used (often innocently) in ways they were not intended to be used. Stalked by a killer, Sarah Conner cannot get through to the police because the nearest phone is out of order. When she finally reaches the LAPD emergency line, on a phone in the Tech Noir nightclub, it is predictably to hear, "All our lines are busy . . . please hold. . . ." Neither can she get through to her roommate, Ginger, to warn her because Ginger and her boyfriend have put on the answering machine while they make love. But Ginger wouldn't have been able to hear the phone, in any case, because she'd worn her Walkman to bed. Tech turns noir again when the Terminator, not Ginger, takes the answering machine message that gives away Sarah's location. Later Sarah will again reveal her whereabouts when the Terminator perfectly mimics her mother's voice over the phone. And in one of the film's most pointed gestures toward the unintentionally harmful effects of technology, the police psychiatrist fails to see the Terminator entering the station when his beeper goes off and distracts him just as their paths cross. Lacking any warning, scores of policemen are killed and the station destroyed. The film seems to suggest that if technology can go wrong or be abused, it will. To illustrate this maxim further, Kyle Reese is shown having a nightmare of his future world where laser-armed, hunter-killed machines track down the few remaining humans; he wakes to hear a radio ad promoting laser-disk stereos. It comes as no surprise, finally, to see that his futuristic concentration camp number is the ubiquitous bar code stamped on today's consumer items.

That tech turns noir because of human decision-making and not something inherent in technology itself is presented even more forcefully in the "novelization" of *The Terminator* by Randall Frakes and Bill Wisher.[3] The novelization adds a twist, perhaps one that originally appeared in the script but was discarded because it would have generated a complicated and digressive subplot. Or perhaps the authors of the book made it up on their own, unable to resist pointing out, once again, that it is humans, not machines, that will bring on the apocalypse. Near the end of the book, after the Terminator has been destroyed, a man named Jack, a Steve Wozniak-like computer prodigy, discovers a microchip in the debris. His entrepreneur friend, Greg, decides that they will go into business for themselves, once they figure out how to exploit what they take to be a new kind of microprocessing unit. Sixteen months later, they incorporate under the name Cyberdyne Systems . . . the company that goes on to make the same defense network computer that will try to destroy humanity in Reese's day. Here the case is being made not so much against the tunnel vision of corporate greed, but against the supposedly more benign coupling of golly-gosh tech-nerd enthusiasm with all-American entrepreneurship.

The film, moreover, does not advance an "us against them" argument, man versus machine, a Romantic opposition between the organic and the mechanical, for there is much that is hybrid about its constructed elements. The Terminator, after all, is part machine, part human—a cyborg. (Its chrome skeleton with its hydraulic muscles and tendons of flexible cable looks like the Nautilus machines Schwarzenegger uses to build his body.) And Kyle's kills as a guerilla fighter are dependent upon his tech abilities—hot-wiring cars, renovating weapons, making bombs. If Kyle has himself become a fighting machine in order to attack the oppressor machines, Sarah too becomes increasingly machine-like as she acquires the skills she needs to survive both the Terminator and the apocalypse to come. The concluding irony is that Kyle and Sarah use machines to distract and then destroy the Terminator when he corners them in a robot-automated factory. At the end of one of the most harrowing, and gruelingly paced, chase scenes on film, Sarah terminates the Terminator between two plates of a hydraulic press. This interpenetration of human and machine is seen most vividly, however, when Sarah is wounded in the thigh by a piece of exploding Terminator shrapnel. Leaving aside the rich history of sexual connotations of wounding in the thigh,[4] part of a machine is here literally incorporated into Sarah's body ("a kind of cold rape," the novelization calls it). While the film addresses an ultimate battle between humans and machines, it nonetheless accepts the impossibility of clearly distinguishing between them. It focuses on the partial and ambiguous merging of the two, a more complex response, and one typical of the critical dystopia, than the Romantic triumph of the organic over the mechanical, or the nihilistic recognition that we have all become automata (even if those automata are better than we are, more human than humans, as in *Blade Runner*).[5]

Time Travel

The Terminator, however, is as much about time as it is about machines. Because cinema itself has the properties of a time machine, it lends itself easily to time travel stories, one of the staples of science fiction literature. Surprisingly, however, there have been relatively few attempts in film to create stories around the idea of time travel. Hollywood, to be sure, has always been more drawn to conquering space and fighting off alien invaders than thinking through the heady paradoxes of voyaging through time. The exceptions have been very successful, however, and so it is curious that the industry has not made more effort to produce such stories. George Pal's *The Time Machine* (1960) was so exquisite (it brought the MGM look to science fiction film) that one even forgave the film's suppression of H. G. Wells's kooky class analysis of the Eloi and the Morlocks, which was, after all, the conceptual center of the original tale. And the runaway success of the banal and clumsily made *Back to the Future* should have convinced Hollywood that there is something commercially attractive about the idea of time travel. Indeed, *The Terminator*'s appeal is due in large part to the way it is able to put to work this classical science fiction theme.

Compared to the complexity of many literary science fiction time travel plots, *The Terminator*'s story is simple: in 2010 a killer cyborg is sent back to the present day with the mission of exterminating Sarah Conner, a part-time waitress and student, the future mother of John Conner, the man who will lead the last remnants of humanity to victory over the machines which are trying to rid the world of humans. John Conner chooses Kyle Reese, a young and hardened fighter, to travel back in time to save Sarah from the Terminator. If the Terminator succeeds in his mission, John Conner, of course, will never be born, and the humans will never be able to fight back successfully against the machines. Kyle has fallen in love with Sarah through her photograph, given to him by John Conner. He says he always wondered what she was thinking about when the photo was taken for she has a faraway look on her face and a sad smile. "I came across time for you," he professes, "I love you. I always have." They make love; he is killed soon after; Sarah destroys the Terminator and leaves for the mountains to give birth to her son and wait out the holocaust to come. The film ends South of the Border with a Mexican boy taking a Polaroid of Sarah as she is thinking of Kyle. It is the photograph that John Conner will give to Kyle, forty years later, knowing that he is sending his own father to his death.

This sort of story is called a time-loop paradox because cause and effect are not only reversed but put into a circle: the later events are caused by the earlier events, and the earlier by the later.[6] If John Conner had not sent Kyle Reese back in time to be his father, he would never have been born. But he was born, so Kyle Reese must *already* have traveled back to the past to impregnate Sarah Conner. As another instance of paradox, John Conner's fighting skills were taught him by his mother. Sarah Conner, however, learned those skills from Kyle Reese, who had himself learned them while fighting at John Conner's side. (The novelization adds another time-loop paradox in locating the origin of the defense network computer in the microchip found in the Terminator debris.) Small wonder then that Sarah looks slightly bewildered when Kyle says he has "always loved" her. How could this be true when, from the perspective of her point in time, he hasn't been born yet?

What is the appeal of time loop paradox stories? They are so fascinating that many people who used to read science fiction but have long since given it up will usually remember one story in particular, Ray Bradbury's "A Sound of Thunder," even if they can no longer recall the author or the title (others have also noted this phenomenon). In this famous story, big-game hunters from the future travel back to the age of dinosaurs. They don't have to fear that their shooting and bagging will affect the future, however, because dinosaurs will soon be extinct anyway. They are strictly warned, though, not to step off the walkway that has been prepared for them over the primeval jungle. One hunter disobeys and in doing so crushes a tiny butterfly under his boot. When the hunting party returns to the future, everything is ever so slightly different, the result of killing one small insect million of years earlier.

Primal Scene

The essential elements of time travel and its consequences are witnessed in a very succinct way in "A Sound of Thunder." That is why the story is remembered. But when plots of this kind become more complex, one theme tends to predominate: what would it be like to go back in time and give birth to oneself? Or, what would it be like to be one's own mother and father? Robert Heinlein has given us the seminal treatment of this paradoxical situation in "All You Zombies." A time traveler who has undergone a sex-change operation not only encounters both earlier and later versions of himself but turns out to be his own mother and father. Similarly, in David Gerrold's *The Man Who Folded Himself*, each time the protagonist travels in time, he reduplicates himself. Eventually this results in a large group of identical men who find each other to be ideal lovers. One of them goes very far back in time and meets a lesbian version of himself. They fall in love, have children, and then break up, to return to their copy-lovers. (As the narrator says in "All You Zombies," "It's a shock to have it proved to you that you can't resist seducing yourself.") The appeal of *Back to the Future* should now be apparent—it is only a more vulgar version of the desire manifested in these stories. There is of course a name for this desire; it is called a primal scene fantasy, the name Freud gave to the fantasy of overhearing or observing parental intercourse, of being on the scene, so to speak, of one's own conception. The desire represented in the time travel story, of both witnessing one's own conception and being one's own mother and father, is similar to the primal scene fantasy, in which one can be both observer or one of the participants. (The possibility of getting pregnant and giving birth to oneself is echoed in *Back to the Future*'s TV ad: "The first kid to get into trouble before he was ever born.") The reconstruction of a patient's primal scene assumes, in fact, a great deal of time travel. (Freud said the most extreme primal scene fantasy was that of observing parental intercourse while one is still an unborn baby in the womb.)[7] The Wolf-Man, supine on the analytic couch, is sent further and further back in time to "remember" the moment when, as a child, he saw his parents having sex. Although Freud's interpretation depends upon the Wolf-man witnessing such a scene, he decides, finally, that it was not necessary for the event to have *actually occurred* for it to have had profound effects on the patient's psychical life. A patient can consciously fabricate such a scene only because it has been operative in his or her unconscious, and this construction has nothing to do with its actual occurrence or nonoccurrence. The idea of returning to the past to generate an event that has already made an impact on one's identity, lies at the core of the time-loop paradox story.

What is *The Terminator*'s primal scene? The last words that Kyle Reese throws at the Terminator, along with a pipe bomb, are "Come on, motherfucker!" But in the narrative logic of this film it is Kyle who is the mother fucker. And within the structure of fantasy that shapes the film, John Conner is the child who orchestrates his own primal scene, one inflected by a family romance, moreover, because his is able to choose his own father, singling out Kyle from the other soldiers. That such a fantasy is an attempted end-run around Oedipus is also obvious: John

Conner can identify with his father, can even *be* his father in the scene of parental intercourse, and also conveniently dispose of him in order to go off with (in) his mother.

Recent film theory has taken up Freud's description of fantasy to give a more complete account of how identification works in film.[8] An important emphasis has been placed on the subject's ability to assume, successively, all the available positions in the fantasmatic scenario. Extending this idea to film has shown that spectatorial identification is more complex than has hitherto been understood because it shifts constantly in the course of the film's narrative, while crossing the lines of biological sex; in other words, unconscious identification with the characters or the scenario is not necessarily dependent upon gender. Another element of Freud's description of fantasy that also deserves attention, particularly in discussing fantasy in relation to popular film, is the self-serving or wish-fulfilling aspect of fantasy. In "The Paths to the Formation of Symptoms," Freud constructs two analogies between the creation of fantasy and instances drawn from "real life." He begins by saying that a child uses fantasies to disguise the history of his childhood, "just as every nation disguises its forgotten prehistory by constructing legends" (p. 368). A fantasy is thus not "just a fantasy" but a story *for* the subject. The fantasy of seduction, for example, serves to deny the subject's acts of autoeroticism by projecting them onto another person. (Such fantasy constructions, Freud says, should be seen separately from those real acts of adult seduction of children that occur more frequently than is acknowledged.) Similarly, in the "family romance" the subject creates another parent, an ideal one, to make up for the perceived shortcomings of the real mother or father. Thus a film like *The Terminator* that is so clearly working in relation to a primal fantasy, is also working in the service of pleasure (already a requirement for a mass audience film), a pleasure that depends upon suppressing conflicts or contradictions. (Because such suppression does not always work, and because desire does not always aim for pleasure—the death drive—much recent film analysis is devoted to examining those aspects of film that go distinctly "beyond the pleasure principle.")[9]

Take, for example, the seemingly contradictory figure of Kyle Reese. The film "cheats" with his image in the same way that *The Searchers* "cheats" with Martin Pauley's image, which is, variously, wholly Indian, "half-breed," "quarter-blood" Cherokee, one-eighth Cherokee, or wholly white, depending upon the unconscious and ideological demands of the narrative at any given moment.[10] In *The Terminator* Kyle is the virile, hardened fighter barking orders to the terrified Sarah, but alternately he is presented as boyish, vulnerable, and considerably younger in appearance than her. His childishness is underscored by Sarah's increasingly maternal affection for him (bandaging his wounds, touching his scars); and in the love scene, he is the young man being initiated by the more experienced, older woman. Kyle is thus both the father of John Conner and, in his youth and inexperience, Sarah's son, John Conner. The work of fantasy allows the fact of incest to be both stated and dissimulated. It is only in fantasy, finally, that we can have our cake and eat it too. Or as the French equivalent puts it, even more aptly, that we can be and have been—*peut être et avoir été.*

Freud also compared the mental realm of fantasy to a "reservation" or "nature reserve," a place set aside where:

> the requirements of agriculture, communication and industry threaten to bring about changes in the original face of the earth which will quickly make it unrecognizable [almost a description of a post- apocalyptic landscape]. Everything, including what is useless and even what is noxious, can grow and proliferate there as it pleases. The mental realm of fantasy is just such a reservation withdrawn from the reality principle [p. 372].

Can a film like *The Terminator* be similarly dismissed as merely escapist, appealing as it does to a realm of fantasy "withdrawn from the reality principle," where even our incestuous desires can be realized? For one possible answer we can turn to the end of Freud's essay on symptom formation, where he tells us that there is "a path that leads back from fantasy to reality—the path, that is, of art." An artist, he says, has the ability to shape a faithful image of his fantasy, and then to depersonalize and generalize it so that it is made accessible to other people. Even if we do not have as much faith in "art" or the "artist" as Freud has, we can still draw some useful conclusions from what he says.

One could argue that *The Terminator* treads the path from fantasy back to reality precisely because it is able to generalize its vision, to offer something more than this fully, though paradoxically, resolved primal fantasy. This *generalizing* of the fantasy is carried out through *The Terminator*'s use of the topical and everyday: as we have seen, the film's texture is woven from the technological litter of modern life. But this use of the topical is not, for example, like *E.T.*'s more superficial referencing of daily life through brand name kid-speak, that is, topicality for topicality's sake. Rather, it is a dialogue with Americana that bespeaks the inevitable consequences of our current technological addictions. To give another example, the shopping mall in George Romero's *Dawn of the Dead* is more than a kitsch ambience, it is a way of concretely demonstrating the zombification of consumer culture. By exposing every corner of the mall—stores, escalators, public walkways, basement, roof—the location becomes saturated with meaning, in a way that goes far beyond *E.T.*'s token gesturing toward the commodification of modern life. If *The Terminator*'s primal scene fantasy draws the spectator into the film's paradoxical circle of cause and effect and its equally paradoxical realization of incestuous desire, its militant everydayness throws the spectator back out again, back to the technological future.

Science Fiction and Sexual Difference

In the realm of the unconscious and fantasy, the question of the subject's origin, "Where do I come from?" is followed by the question of sexual difference, "Who am I (What sex am I)?" It is by now well known that the narrative logic of classical film is powered by the desire to establish, by the end of the film, the nature of masculinity, the nature of femininity, and the way in which those two can be complementary rather than antagonistic.[11] But in film and television, as elsewhere, it is becoming increasingly difficult to *tell the difference.* As men and women are less and less differentiated by a division of labor, what, in fact, makes them different? And how can classical film still construct the difference so crucial to its formula for narrative closure? Ironically, it is science fiction film—our hoariest and seemingly most sexless genre—that alone remains capable of supplying the configurations of sexual difference required by the classical cinema. If there is increasingly less practical difference between men and women, there is more than enough difference between a human and an alien (*The Man Who Fell to Earth, Starman*), a human and a cyborg/replicant (*Android, Blade Runner*), or a human from the present and one from the future (*The Terminator*). In these films the question of sexual difference—a question whose answer is no longer "self-evident"—is displaced onto the more remarkable difference between the human and the other. That this questioning of the difference between the human and the other is sexual in nature, can also be seen in the way these films reactivate infantile sexual investigation. One of the big questions for the viewer of *Blade Runner*, for example, is "How do replicants do *it*?" Or, of *The Man Who Fell to Earth*, "What is the sex of this alien who possesses nothing that resembles human genitals (its sex organs are in its hands)?"

But if recent science fiction film provides the heightened sense of difference necessary to the classical narrative, it also offers the reassurance of difference *itself.* In describing one important aspect of the shift in the psychical economy from the nineteenth century to the twentieth century, Raymond Bellour maintains that in the nineteenth century men looked at women and feared they were different, but in the twentieth century men look at women and fear they are the same.[12] The majority of science fiction films work to dissipate that fear of the same, to ensure that there is a difference. A very instructive example is the NBC miniseries *V*, broadcast during the 1983–84 season. A rare instance of science fiction on television (*Star Trek* to the contrary, the television industry insists that science fiction does not work on television), *V* tried to be as topical and up-to-date as possible, particularly in the roles it gave to women. The Commander of the alien force that takes over Earth's major cities, the Supreme commander of the aliens, the leader of the Earthling guerrillas, and the leader of the alien fifth column aiding the Earthlings, are all played by women. They are seen performing the same activities as the men (planning, fighting, counterattacking, infiltrating, etc.), thus removing the most important visible signs of difference. The only difference remaining in *V* is that between the aliens (scaly, green reptiles in human disguise) and the humans. That difference, however, comes to represent sexual difference, as if the alien/human difference were a projection of what can no longer be depicted otherwise.[13] The leader of the guerrillas is captured and brainwashed by the alien commander. Although she is eventually rescued by her comrades, it is feared that the brainwashing has turned her into an alien. She even begins using her left hand rather than her right one, a reptile-alien characteristic. Thus when she and her boyfriend, the second in command of the guerrillas, are shown making love, we realize, as they do, that this could be interspecies sex—the blond, all-American Julie may be a lizard underneath it all, whether in fact or in mind. It gives the otherwise banal proceedings a powerful source of dramatic tension, while it reassures TV-viewing audiences everywhere that there is a difference. (Such a radical disposition of difference always risks, of course, tipping over into the horror of too *much* difference.)

Similarly, it is instructive to see how *Aliens*, directed by James Cameron following his success with *The Terminator*, cracks under the strain of trying to keep to the very original *lack* of sexual differentiation in its precursor, Ridley Scott's *Alien* (not counting, of course, the penultimate scene of Ripley in her bikini underwear). Dan O'Bannon's treatment for the first film was unique in writing each role to be played by either a man or a woman.[14] Ridley Scott's direction followed through on this idea, producing a film that is (for the most part) stunningly egalitarian. In attempting to repeat the equal-opportunity camaraderie of the first film, Cameron's sequel includes a mixed squad of marines, in which the women are shown to be as tough as the men, maybe tougher. And Ripley is, again, the bravest and smartest member of the team. But this time there is a difference, one that is both improbable and symptomatic. Ripley "develops" a maternal instinct, risking her life to save the little girl who is the only survivor of a group of space colonists decimated by the aliens. Tenaciously protective, she takes on the mother alien, whose sublime capacity for destruction is shown nonetheless to result from the same kind of maternal love that Ripley exhibits. Ripley is thus marked by a difference that is automatically taken to be a sign of femininity. (We do not see Hicks, for example—played by Michael Biehn, who was Kyle Reese in *The Terminator*—acting irrationally in order to rescue a child who is probably already dead.) *Aliens* reintroduces the issue of sexual difference, but not in order to offer a newer, more modern configuration of that difference. Rather, by focusing on Ripley alone (Hicks is awkwardly "disappeared" from the film in the closing moments), the question of the couple is supplanted by the problem of the woman as mother. What we get finally is a conservative moral lesson about maternity, futuristic or otherwise: mothers will be mothers, and they will *always* be women. We can conclude that even when there is not much sex in science fiction, there is nonetheless a great deal about sexuality, here reduced to phallic motherhood: Ripley in the robot-expediter is simply the Terminator turned inside out.

Just as it is ironic that science fiction film can give us the sharper notion of sexual difference lost from contemporary classical film, so too it is ironic that when this genre does depict sexual activity, it offers some of the most effective instances of eroticism in recent film. The dearth of eroticism in current filmmaking is pointed up by Woody Allen's success in providing the paradigm of the only kind of sexual difference we have left: the incompatibility of the man's neuroses with the woman's neuroses. Understandably, this is not very erotic. But science fiction film, in giving us an extreme version of sexual difference, coincides with the requirements of the erotic formula, one which describes a fantasy of absolute difference and absolute complementarity (the quality of being complementary, of course, depending upon the establishment of difference). Unlike in classical cinema, the science fiction couple is often not the product of a long process of narrative differentiation; rather, the man and the woman are different *from the very beginning*. The narrative can then focus on *them together* and the *exterior* obstacles they must overcome to remain a couple. The erotic formula has, in fact, two parts: first, the two members of the couple must be marked as clearly different. (In non-science fiction film, for example, she is a nun, he is a priest; she is white, he is black, she is a middle-class widow, he is a young working-class man; she is French, he is German/Japanese, etc.) Second, one of the two must die or at least be threatened by death. If the man and the woman, in their absolute difference, are absolutely complementary, then there is nothing left to be desired. Something has to be taken away to regenerate desire and the narrative. Thus, although the lovemaking scene in *The Terminator* is not a very distinguished one in terms of the relatively perfunctory way that it was filmed, it nonetheless packs a strong erotic charge, *in its narrative context* because it is a kiss across time, a kiss between a man from the future and a woman from the present, an act of love pervaded by death. For Kyle has to die in order to justify the coda, in which Sarah ensures the continuity of the story, now a legend of their love for each other.

Time Travel as Primal Scene: La Jetée

If time travel stories are fantasies of origins, they are also fantasies of endings. Mark Rose has pointed out that many of the narratives that deal with time travel tend to be fictions of apocalypse.[15] As in *The Terminator*, however, these visions of endings may also be visions of new beginnings—in the Genesis version, after God destroys the world by flood, it is Sarah who is anointed "mother of all nations." Rose cites Frank Kermode's *The Sense of an Ending* to show that we create fictions of endings to give meaning to time, to transform *chronos*—mere passing time—into *kairos*, time invested with the meaning derived from its goal. History is given shape, is made understandable by spatializing time, by seeing it as a line along which one can travel. Such spatialization of time, however, introduces the paradox of time travel. "Much of the fascination of the time loop is related to the fact that it represents the point at which the spatialization of time breaks down" (Rose, p. 108). If I could travel back into the past, I could (theoretically) murder my own grandmother. But I would cease to exist. How then could I have murdered her?

If this example illustrates the collapse of time as we know it, it also shows that it is impossible to separate ourselves from time. (The time traveler who murders her grandmother ceases to exist.) Thus time travel paradox narratives typically explore either the question of the end of time or the reciprocal relation between ourselves and time (Rose, p. 108). Although *The Terminator* is concerned with both apocalypse and the question of time in relation to personal identity, another film which preceded it by more than 20 years, Chris Marker's *La Jetée*, weaves the two together in a way that still haunts the spectator of this stunning film. *The Terminator*, in fact, bears such an uncanny resemblance to *La Jetée* that Cameron's film could almost be its mass-culture remake. Marker's film too is about a post-apocalyptic man who is chosen to be a time traveller because of his fixation of an image of the past. It too involves a love affair between a woman from the present and a man from the future, and an attempt to keep humanity from being wiped out.

A crucial difference between *The Terminator* and *La Jetée*, however, is that Marker's film explicitly addresses the paradox of time travel. After being sent on numerous journeys through time, *La Jetée*'s time traveller attempts to return to the scene from his childhood that had marked him so deeply. On that day, a Sunday afternoon before a third World War which will drive the few remaining survivors underground, his parents had brought him to Orly to watch the planes take off. He remembers seeing the sun fixed in the sky, a scene at the end of the jetty, and a woman's face. Then, a sudden noise, the woman's gesture, a crumbling body, the cries of the crowd. Later, the voice-over tells us, he knew that he had seen a man die. When he tries to return to that Sunday at Orly, he is killed by one of the scientists from the underground camp who had sent him voyaging through time; they no longer have any use for him. The moment, then, that he had been privileged to see as a child and which had never stopped haunting him, was the moment of his own death. In the logic of this film he has to die, because such a logic acknowledges the temporal impossibility of being in the same place as both adult and child. In *La Jetée* one cannot be and have been.

The film goes even further when it insists on the similar paradox at work in the primal scene fantasy by depicting the psychical consequence of attempting to return to a scene from one's childhood: such a compulsion to repeat, and the regression that it implies, leads to the annihilation of the subject.[16] But the subject is also extinguished in another way, this time through a symbolic castration depicted as a very real death.

The woman he is searching for is at the end of the jetty, but so is the man whose job it is to prevent him from possessing her, the man and the woman on the jetty mirroring the parental (Oedipal) couple that brought the little boy to the airport. (This film's version of the Terminator succeeds in its mission.) While *The Terminator* gives us a time travel story that depends upon a primal scene fantasy for its unconscious appeal, its fantasmatic force. *La Jetée* shows that the two are one and the same: the fantasy of time travel is no more nor less than the compulsion to repeat that manifests itself in the primal scene fantasy. Moreover, since *La Jetée*'s circular narrative is wholly organized as a "beginning toward which [one] is constantly moving,"[17] it suggests that all film viewing is infantile sexual investigation.

The Terminator, in many respects, merely abstracts and reifies *La Jetée*'s major elements. Marker's film, for example, is composed almost entirely of still images, photographs that dissolve in and out of one another in a way that constantly edges toward the illusion of "real" filmic movement. As Thierry Kuntzel has pointed out,[18] such a technique allows *La Jetée* to be a film about movement in film, and our desire for movement. Using still images to make a film is also a perfect way to tell a time travel story because it offers the possibility of mixing two different temporalities: the "pastness" of the photographic image and the "here-nowness" of the illusionistic (filmic) movement.[19]

Although I suggested that *The Terminator* could be seen as the industry remake of *La Jetée*, it should now be clear that Marker's film could not be remade because in its very structure it is *unrepeatable*. Inasmuch as it acknowledges the paradox of the time loop and rejects the rosy nostalgia of a wish- fulfilling version of the primal scene fantasy, it is not likely remake material with respect to popular film's demand for pleasure without (obvious) paradox. Similarly, one could not imagine a *sequel* to *La Jetée* because of the way the film collapses time in its rigorous observance of the fatalistic logic of time travel. But one can be sure that *Terminators* is already more than a gleam in a producer's eye. After all, what is to stop John Conner, in another possible future, from sending Kyle Reese back in time again, but at a later date, perhaps so that he could rendezvous with Sarah in her South of the Border hide-out?

Would it not be too easy, however, to conclude by pitting *La Jetée* against *The Terminator*? To end by falling back on less-than-useful dichotomies like the avant-garde versus Hollywood or even the Symbolic versus the Imaginary? It is true that *La Jetée* is governed by "the laws of recollection and symbolic recognition" (in Lacan's terms) while *The Terminator* is reuled by "the laws of imaginary reminiscence."[20] But it is precisely the way *The Terminator* harnesses the power of "imaginary reminiscence" (the primal scene fantasy of time travel) that allows it to present one of the most forceful of recent science fiction tales about the origins of techno-apocalypse. The film is able to do so, as I have argued, by generalizing its core of fantasy through the systematic use of the topical and everyday, reminding us that the future is now. As a critical dystopia, *The Terminator* thus goes beyond the flashy nihilism of apocalypse-for-the-sake-of-apocalypse to expose a more *mundane* logic of technological modernity, even if it is one that is, finally, no less catastrophic.

Notes

1. Fredric Jameson, "Progress Versus Utopia; or Can We Imagine the Future?" *Science Fiction Studies* 9 (1982).
2. Stanislaw Lem, "Cosmology and Science Fiction," trans. Franz Rottenstein, *Science Fiction Studies* 4 (1977): 109.
3. Randall Frakes and Bill Wisher, *The Terminator* (New York: Bantam Books, 1984). (A novel based on the screenplay by James Cameron with Gale Anne Hurd).
4. See Jessie L. Weston, *From Ritual to Romance: An Account of the Holy Grail from Ancient Ritual to Christian Symbol* (Cambridge: Cambridge University Press, 1920), pp. 42–48.
5. For a full and very interesting discussion of the political dimensions of the cyborg, see Donna Harraway. "A Manifesto for Cyborgs: Science, Technology, and Socialist Feminism in the 1980s," *Socialist Review*, no. 80 (March-April, 1985).
6. Useful essays on time travel and its paradoxes include Stanislaw Lem, "The Time-Travel Story and Related Matters of SF Structuring," *Science Fiction Studies* 1, 1974; Monte Cook, "Tips for Time Travel," *Philosophers Look at Science Fiction* (Chicago: Nelson-Hall, 1982); and David Lewis, "The Paradoxes of Time Travel," *Thought Probes*, eds. Fred D. Miller, Jr. and Nicholas D. Smith (New Jersey: Prentice Hall, 1981).
7. Sigmund Freud, "The Paths to the Formation of Symptoms," *The Standard Edition of the Complete Psychological Works of Sigmund Freud*, ed. and trans. James Strachey (London: Hogarth Press, 1958) 16:370.
8. See, among others, Elisabeth Lyon, "The Cinema of Lol V. Stein," *Camera Obscura* no. 6 (1980); Elizabeth Cowie, "Fantasia," *m/f* no. 9 (1984); and Steve Neale, "Sexual Difference in Cinema," *Sexual Difference*, special issue of *The Oxford Literary Review* 8, nos. 1–2 (1986).
9. For the best formulation of this idea, see Joan Copjec, "*India Song/Son nom de Venise dans Calcutta désert:* The Compulsion to Repeat," *October* 17 (Summer 1981).
10. Brian Henderson, "The Searchers: An American Dilemma," *Film quarterly* 34, no. 2 (Winter 1980–1981); reprinted in *Movies and Methods*, ed. Bill Nichols (Berkeley: University of California Press, 1985), vol. 2.

11. There are, of course, important exceptions to this standard narrative logic, as Jacqueline Rose has shown, for example, in her analysis of *The Birds*, in which Mitch's "successful" attainment of a masculine and paternal identity comes at the price of regression and catatonia for Melanie. "Paranoia and the Film System," *Screen* 17, no. 4 (Winter 1976–1977).

12. Raymond Bellour, "Un jour, la castration," *L'Arc*, no. 71 (1978) (special issue on Alexandre Dumas).

13. This wholly unremarkable series seems surprisingly capable of taking on a great deal of cultural resonance in its radical presentation of "difference." Andrew Kopkind (*The Nation* 243, no. 17, Nov. 22, 1986) reports that *V* is currently one of the most popular shows in South Africa. He speculates that the show's success lies in the unconsciously ironic, allegorical reading that it allows. Kopkind cites the newspaper description of the week's episode (broadcast on the state-controlled television channel): "TV 4: 9:03. 'Visitor's Choice.' The Resistance stages a daring attack at a convention of Visitor Commanders where Diana intends to show off the ultimate device in processing humans for food."

Robit Hairman in *The Voice* (Jan. 13, 1987) also reports on the cult that has grown up around *V* in South Africa because of the allegorical readings that escaped the government censors. Before the series was over, anti-government forces were spraying slogans from the series on walls in Johannesburg and Soweto, and T-shirts with a large V painted on front and back became a feature on the streets: "*V* joined the mythology of the resistance."

There are also at least two fanzines devoted to *V*, the newest of which, *The Resistance Chronicles*, describes its first issue in terms that evoke infantile sexual investigation: "This volume will contain the answers to the following burning questions – Why is that blue Chevy with the fogged-up windows rocking back and forth??? How does Chris Farber feel about virtue . . . and boobs? What color underwear does Ham Tyler wear? What do Ham and Chris keep in their medicine cabinet? Plus a musical *V* parody, 'We're off to See the Lizard . . .' " Description taken from *Dutazine*, no. 44 (Oct.-Nov. 1986).

14. Danny Peary reports this in his interview with Sigourney Weaver, "Playing Ripley in *Alien*," *OMNI's Screen Flights/Screen Fantasies: The Future According to Science Fiction Cinema*, ed. Danny Peary (Garden City, N.Y.: Doubleday, 1984) 162.

15. Mark Rose, *Alien Encounters: Anatomy of Science Fiction* (Cambridge, Mass.: Harvard University Press, 1981) 99.

16. My discussion of primal scene fantasy in *La Jetée* is indebted to Thierry Kuntzel's lectures on that topic in his 1975–1976 seminar at the American University Center for Film Studies in Paris.

17. Ned Lukacher's formulation of the primal scene fantasy in *Primal Scenes: Literature, Philosophy, Psychoanalysis* (Ithaca: Cornell University Press, 1986), p. 42. This book contains the best recent discussion of the structure of the primal scene fantasy.

18. In his lectures on *La Jetée* at the American University Center for Film Studies.

19. The distinction is made by Roland Barthes in "Rhetoric of the Image," *Image – Music – Text*, trans. Stephen Heath (New York: Hill and Wang, 1977) 45.

20. Jacques Lacan, *Ecrits: A Selection* (New York: Norton, 1977) 141. A distinction cited by Lukacher, 43.

Ethical Dimensions of the Postmodern

STEPHEN MELVILLE

WE ARE MEETING HERE UNDER THE TITLE "CULTURAL POLITICS OF POSTMODERNism," and I want my remarks to unfold as something of a prolonged hesitation over this title. It marks to a high degree the current position of the question of postmodernism, and is to that degree problematic for a thought that sees the postmodern as itself a questioning of the notion of "position."

This title offers, at least grammatically, the possibility of any number of other such meetings—cultural politics of the Renaissance, for example, or, conversely, the political economy of postmodernism. But this grammatical promise is in important ways false. The "cultural politics of postmodernism" does not primarily arise from the coupling of some more or less disciplinary pursuit with one era among others in some periodized history. The phrase "cultural politics of postmodernism" functions now primarily as a way of naming the postmodern as a certain coincidence of the realms of culture and politics ("cultural politics" is itself the name of a period). Over the course of a very few years the phrase "cultural politics of postmodernism" has come to name as well a certain presumed coalescence of theory around its historical moment, a "subject-position" and a theory of "subject-positions": "postmodernism" is at once a kind of theory (theory freed from the constraints through which theory is traditionally defined) and the object or condition grasped by that theory.

There is now about the postmodern and our theoretical grasp of it a kind of closure that was perhaps more difficult to imagine even as little as five years ago: things, in theory and in criticism, have been settled, usages regularized. For me this double domestication of theory and of the postmodern has been somewhat unnerving, perhaps even alarming; my remarks today may thus seem to be somewhat reactionary. They are I hope at least not merely reactive.

The line of talk that sees in postmodernism an essentially political tendency is by now quite well-established. My purpose is not quite to quarrel with this approach, but I do want to sketch out another tendency at work as well, one that is frequently read as a certain resistance to politics, that often sets itself forward through an appeal to "ethics," and that is marked by a continuing interest in "formalist" questions and topics. I have placed both "ethics" and "formalist" within quotation marks here, and what I hope to do in this talk is unpack the necessity of that bracketing—and of the bracketing this would, in its turn, impose on the word "politics." I am uncertain in particular about my ability to deliver on this word "ethics." I will in a sense do little more than point to the places where it seems to me to demand to be spoken; whatever it is that compels that speech does not, I think, take the form of "an ethics" that might be opposed to or take the place of "a politics."[1] I am, I suppose, interested in making out, or teasing out, a difference between seeing in the postmodern a political stance and seeing in it a worry about the terms and structures through which one recognizes or acknowledges a position as political. Perhaps more simply, I am interested in what I can make out of the various imperatives that motivate or figure in my own writing on things postmodern.

There are two primary ways of glossing the phrase "cultural politics." On perhaps the more frequent argument, at least in American circles, postmodernity is the becoming explicitly political of culture—and the eye of postmodern theory finds implicit politics where and whenever it finds culture. "Cultural politics" is thus understood as a particular theoretical *donnée* that can be turned back upon the range of earlier eras and engender new analyses and interpretations of them (thus making real in its way the promise of a conference on the cultural politics of the Renaissance). Most versions of this reading depend upon a larger teleological frame, sometimes concealed and sometimes overt.

There is another reading of this phrase, more "European" perhaps, in which the emphasis falls on the becoming cultural of politics, not a rediscovery of the political in a new place but its appropriation to something else. This would mark a major historical shift in the meaning of politics itself. For some this shift means precisely a loss of the political, but others find in it an extraordinary means to authorizing their every gesture as inherently political and consequential. The first reading, the one that sees culture becoming political, tends to root itself in Marx; the second tends to think itself beyond Marx and is associated perhaps most closely with such figures as Jean-François Lyotard and Jean Baudrillard. Since both views can be united through the assertion that "now everything is political," the line between them is often fuzzy, and sometimes invisible.

I do not want to take sides in this dispute, although it will be clear enough that one will not say what I am trying to say unless the alternative represented by Lyotard and Baudrillard has already struck one as, perhaps permanently, powerful and tempting. I am interested in the fact of the double reading and in trying to say something about the necessity of the difference between them.

The issue here is frequently put in terms of a question of representation: the Marxist continues to hold to a notion of representation as, at least, a regulating ideal if not finally a realizable possibility, even as he or she is increasingly tempted to equate representation with ideology *tout court* (thus, for example, Jameson's complex and ultimately self-baffling formulations of history in *The Political Unconscious*); the theorist we might call post-Marxist tends to argue that we have been so thoroughly delivered from presence and so wholly given over to representation as to be beyond the reach of any epistemologically well-grounded regulatory ideal. Caught in the middle, much politically-minded theoretical writing of the past five years or so has tended to a vague appeal to a notion of the simultaneous universality and recognizability of the ideological, often bolstered by appeals to Foucault, Gramsci or Bakhtin, and an insistence, that seems condemned finally to emptiness, on the value of contestatory or interventionist reading. We have thus taken out of the sharply contrasted and carefully developed positions of the 70's a casual notion of some "discursive constitution of the real" that licenses—and stakes—at once everything and nothing. The result can give rise to some weird reading experiences: one finds oneself moving from, say, Catherine Belsey or Kaja Silverman to departmental memos to a *New Yorker* profile of Estée Lauder without leaving the shelter of a presiding vocabulary of ideology, subject, and position—as if the languages of management and left-wing critique had surreptitiously merged. Or one finds enacted within the unity of the Reagan administration the very contrasts in interpretive strategy that are seen as the central issues within literary theory; our left-wing reads as Reagan reads the ABM treaty, our right as Meese reads the Constitution—and wc ought to be left wondering whether we have construed our issues at all correctly. Reagan has succeeded in displacing political questions into matters of management style, and I cannot help wondering if we have not done so as well, under the commodious umbrella of what we have come to call, often oddly, a "critique" or "politics" of "representation."[2]

The origins of this critique are frequently attributed to Heidegger. The irony is that much that Heidegger most feared is now being conducted in some measure under the invocation of his name. One wants to note in the following passages from "The Age of the World Picture" the logic they can reveal working the vicissitudes I am trying to track in the phrase "cultural politics":

> One of the essential phenomena of the modern age is its science. [Heidegger glosses this a page later with: "The essence of what we today call science is research. . . . Through the projecting of the ground plan and the prescribing of rigor, (research) procedure makes secure for itself its sphere of objects within the realm of Being."]
>
> A third equally essential phenomenon of the modern period lies in the event of art's moving into the purview of aesthetics. That means that the art work becomes the object of mere subjective experience, and that consequently art is considered to be an expression of human life.
>
> A fourth modern phenomenon manifests itself in the fact that human activity is conceived and consummated as culture. Thus, culture is the realization of the highest values, through the nurture and cultivation of the highest goods of man. It lies in the essence of culture, as such nurturing, to nurture itself in its turn and thus to become the politics of culture.[3]

The remarks on science and research trace out, I think, the place of too much contemporary theory in relation to the postmodern; the further remarks on aesthetics and culture map the apparently complex and oppositional but finally simple space common to Jameson and Baudrillard. What is perhaps most immediately striking here is the way in which Heidegger sees "aesthetics" as continuous with the claim to its overcoming as life, and sees that claim as always further reversible into an aestheticization of politics. What links the thoughts about science with those about culture is their common submission to a notion of representation bound in a particular way to a notion of presence.

What Heidegger aimed at in trying to contest this drift of the world was not a critique of representation in the sense of an opposition to it, but a critique of the underlying notion of presence that allows representation to surreptitiously substitute for it. What Heidegger feared was a certain simultaneous effacement and perfection of representation that could lead us to inhabit a picture without knowing it or as if that did not matter; his effort to name this risk and its overcoming as "*Ge-stell*," "enframing," is an attempt to restore to us representation *as* representation.[4] I am aware that this is not a usual characterization of Heidegger's interests, but I think it is an important one to advance in a situation in which we have to an extent forgotten what is at stake in talking about representation. Everything here turns in the "as" of "representation as representation." What is in need of critique is, so to speak, our willingness to overlook this particle, our urge to evade the peculiar inward disturbance it provokes in the notion of presence itself. Whether we cast Heidegger's interest in representation as critique or as revalorization, we can grasp its sense only insofar as we see the work it does on the notion of presence. The project is aimed neither at freeing us of representation—nothing can so free us—nor at freeing us to representation *tout court*—because there is no such thing to be freed to (this is the always denied and always revived dream of the Lacanian Symbolic, that we might be, if not subjects among other subjects, then signifiers among other signifiers). To say that everything is representation is to say that we inhabit the world by haunting it, from within a certain distance and marked by the impurity of our finitude—but these terms are perhaps closer to Derrida's continuation of this project and for the moment at least I want to stay nearer Heidegger.

In "The Origin of the Work of Art"[5] Heidegger is, at a certain point, examining the notion of equipment, stuff, and reaches out for a handy example: shoes. And in order to direct our attention he says: for example, the ones in this painting. We are, listening to Heidegger, looking at these shoes. There is nothing between us and them, no frame (we are not looking at a painting; we are looking at shoes). But as Heidegger looks at them and begins to talk about them, something happens: they—themselves unframed—turn out to frame a world—peasant woman's or miner's, it doesn't matter much for now[6]—and so end by showing themselves a work of art. The textual movement here is odd. It is not argumentative; nor is it in any readily recognizable sense a movement from a presentation proper to things to a representation proper to art—although that is the movement for which Heidegger seems to have been preparing us. It is not so much a theoretical movement as it is an enacting of the fate of presence: the point is not that painted shoes differ from real shoes in being framed but that shoes, fully present, hand themselves over to representation—and this handing of themselves over to representation unfolds as a simultaneous framing of the world by the shoes ("from the dark opening of the worn insides . . .") and their enframing within the world (their becoming art). This play on inside and outside has been prepared throughout the essay, relatively apart from the apparent work of the argument, in the lyric effusions it is always tempting to pass over as somehow simply Heidegger's romanticism (as if we know what it means to dismiss the romantic). Heidegger's thought here is not far from Kant—there are ways things in the world come to us such that they show themselves as art—and Derrida, exploring the parergonal logic of *The Critique of Judgement*, makes the link to the question of the frame and its duplicity, at once internal and external to the work, explicit. To grasp the logic of this movement is to begin to see what it means to speak of "representation as representation" and why that can name neither some imaginary moment at which representation "succeeds" in effacing itself utterly nor some equally imaginary moment in which representation becomes purely itself, freed of the burden of that which it would otherwise be said to represent.

In "The Age of the World Picture" Heidegger works toward this acknowledgment of representation rather differently, both more and less explicitly. He writes of a "becoming incalculable" that "remains the invisible shadow that is cast around all things everywhere when man has been transformed into *subiectum* and the world into picture," and asserts that "by means of this shadow the modern world extends itself out into a space withdrawn from representation." This is glossed in an appendix:

> Everyday opinion sees in the shadow only the lack of light, if not light's complete denial. In truth, however, the shadow is a manifest, though impenetrable, testimony to the concealed emitting of light. In keeping with this concept of shadow, we experience the incalculable as that which, withdrawn from representation, is nevertheless manifest in whatever is, pointing to Being, which remains concealed.

An invisible shadow.[7] What distinguishes light from shadow is perhaps just that the shadow is what we can see; an invisible shadow will be indistinguishable from the light unless we can feel our way to imagining light as capable of casting its own shadow. To succeed in this would be precisely to grasp representation as representation, and this would be to succeed also in delivering ourselves from inhabiting a world as subjects set before a picture and, as such, incapable of either inhabiting a world or seeing a picture (we moderns think, of course, that we do both; that is our lucidity, the invisible shadow that opens the world to what Heidegger calls research and what we at least at times seem to mean by theory. This triumph of what we think we mean by representation Heidegger calls "withdrawal from representation").

It is perhaps worth pausing over Heidegger's summary statement of what he takes to be the modern:

> The fundamental event of the modern age is the conquest of the world as picture. The word "picture" now means the structured image that is the creature of man's producing which represents and sets before. In such producing, man contends for the position in which he can be that particular being who gives the measure and draws up guidelines for everything that is. Because this position secures, organizes, and articulates itself as a world view, the modern relationship to that which is, is one that becomes, in its decisive unfolding, a confrontation of world views . . . . Science as research is an absolutely necessary form of this establishing of self in the world; it is one of the pathways upon which the modern age rages toward fulfillment of its essence, with a velocity unknown to the participants.

A central question I mean to be posing today is how far that which we call the postmodern—whether in theory or in its objects—prolongs and how far it breaks with this description of the modern.

Against the reign of lucidity, Heidegger appeals to the "gigantic" and "the incalculable" as the source of the invisible shadow that, if seen or felt, would point beyond the modern. In so doing, he repeats and so points back to the figure with whom his own intellectual struggle is most intimate and intense, Immanuel Kant. He points, in particular, to the sublime of the *Third Critique*.

In many ways, Kant represents the moment of greatest danger for Heidegger; but this, in one of Heidegger's favorite tropes, makes him also the point nearest to surpassing or overcoming that danger. If Kant is, as often for Heidegger, the source of the aestheticism that underpins the dominance of technology and the reduction of world to an object of research, he is necessarily at the same time the site in which that aestheticism can be seen to be something else—something, in Heidegger's terms, saving. Nowhere in Heidegger's writing are the impulses to critique and recovery more closely intertwined than in his readings of Kant. The *Critique of Judgement* exerts an extraordinary pressure on the later writings—to the point that at times Heidegger's voluminous dealings with Neitzsche can seem but a mask for this closer and more intense struggle.

Recent French theory has found itself retracing the forms of this struggle—in different ways Derrida, Lyotard, Nancy, and Lacoue-Labarthe can all be seen as caught up in repeating and perhaps radicalizing Heidegger's appeal to Kant as that which opens simultaneously the possibilities of the modern and the postmodern. The very fact of this submission carries consequences for talking about the postmodern that are at some odds with what I take to be the current state of the question—the arrangement, say, that makes of the cultural politics of postmodernism a question for theory rather than a taking of postmodernism itself—not now a period, not something one enters at a certain time—to be a questioning of theory and our political hopes for it (our hope, more specifically, that through theory we will gain or ground a politics). The possibility that Kant, as modern, is already postmodern threatens to undo our representations of history or, to be more specific once more, demands that we think our representations of history in closer relation to the critique of presence that is transforming our sense of theory. One wants to gloss everything at once here, and I am already so far ahead of myself that there is no harm in saying that this "demand" is an instance of what, in the end, I will call "ethics." One would speak then of "doing justice to the past," and would want to hear this cliché as if it offered us something strange and difficult.

But having gone this far, I want to pull back to Kant and the sublime. There is in the *Third Critique* a separation of two moments, an analysis first of the beautiful and then of the sublime (in fact, of course, there are three moments separated within the critique, but I am not alone in being as yet unprepared to read the critique of teleological judgment.) What we call modernism and trace to Kant assumes this separation; Clement Greenberg, for a central example, means to operate within some sense of the terms of the analytic of the beautiful—what strikes my disinterested eye as the beautiful is in fact the beautiful and so claims universal assent. A somewhat different recent example would be Paul Guyer's magisterial commentary on Kant's judgment of taste, a commentary framed by the assumption that Kant's arguments stand apart from the textual and architectonic frame in which Kant inserts them.[8] I have tried to put this description of Guyer's project in such a way that the continuity between its own aestheticism and theoreticism is apparent. To raise the question of the necessity of the architectonic or textual frame—above all the textual frame offered by an analysis of the sublime precisely as that which disrupts all frames—is to enter, within Kant and within the modern, the space of the postmodern. It may be that we enter this space only through the narrow gate of the modern, but when we do enter it our passage does not take the form of a movement from one era to another. What we may, two hundred years later, take to be such a movement is in fact submitted to a different temporality, is as much a step in as a step out. To grasp this, to write the history this moment calls for, demands our engagement with the complex logics elaborated in Nietzsche's repetition, Heidegger's step back, Derrida's *différance*, Freud's *nachtraglichkeit*, and—I would add—Stanley Cavell's valorization of acknowledgement in the face of the project of knowledge.

I do not now want to engage in the reading of Kant, but I will pause over one minor feature of the *Third Critique*. It is indeed true that, embracing Kant's division of the beautiful and the sublime, we are, at least until the recent past, content to take the criteria of the beautiful to serve for modernism and relegate the sublime to the mere historical interest of Romanticism, the cost of this will be represented in a small heap of textual odds and ends that will be what in Kant is still left of the 18th century. One item in this heap will be the odd (from the point of view that appropriates the sublime to Romanticism) excursus on allegory that closes the discussion of the sublime.[9] In drawing attention to this bit of text, I do not mean to focus on the notion of allegory, insofar as it has seemed at least at times to usefully characterize both postmodernism and its theory, but on the perhaps simpler fact that for Kant an act of writing is the appropriate and perhaps necessary response to the experience which discovers to us our agency: this too points toward the insistence of what I am trying to call "ethics" or "the ethical" (I suppose the difference here is that "ethics" assumes *an* ethics; "the ethical" aims rather at the acknowledgment of a medium). There are different inflections with which we can call such writing an attempt to "represent" that experience: some of these inflections are properly Romantic insofar as we continue to divide the Romantic from the modern; others—this is perhaps Paul de Man's major gift—cause all of that to totter.

There are, of course, different inflections to be given as well to the title under which we meet. I started out by focusing on the terms we are given to think in: "cultural politics," "postmodernism," and, staked in them in complex ways, "theory." I have, I suppose, engaged in a certain resistance to too rapid or sure a reading of these terms precisely in order to raise or renew the stakes for theory. The polemic target is perhaps well described as a certain coalescence between an increasing professionalization of theory and a certain settlement of the question of postmodernism as programmatically political. Against this I have been trying to point toward some of the ways in which this coalescence may seem a retreat from the deepest stakes of a claim to postmodernity as well as a loss of the question of theory as a question of writing.

Another way to put this would be to say that I have assumed the objectivity of the genitive that links the various terms. I have taken the presiding question to be about the cultural politics of the uses of the term postmodern, and tried to insert a certain simultaneous resistance to and acknowledgment of that question through the gap installed by the "of" which allows the title to be articulated at all by offering the one as a "representation" of the other. This formulation points toward an inflection still unexplored, the one that lets us hear postmodernism as that which has a cultural politics rather than or as well as being had by it. To explore the subjective genitive of the title would be to talk about the practices we identify as postmodern or as provoking the recognition of the postmodern. The route I will pursue in the remainder of this paper is, thus, different from that taken in the first part, but in many ways the burden will be the same—that we need two words to name what cultural politics appears to name in one; that ethics haunts politics as the postmodern haunts the modern.

What I want to talk about on this side of the question is the one relay that seems to me to play a crucial role in supporting any sustained and serious discussion of postmodernism: photography.[10] The interest of photography is, in a sense, obvious: photography marks a certain extension of technology into the region of art, an extension that much of our mythology can take only as marking the end of art; it marks also a certain ineradicable intrusion of the real, an intrusion that seems similarly to mark an end or limit; finally, as something we are tempted to call mere reproduction or registration, it seems to put a term to our image of the artist as demiurge, and this too can be taken to point toward a certain end of art. All of these apparent features of photography seem to make it exemplary of the passing of modernist aspirations to transcend or insure itself against the conditions of the world. Photography, particularly as it is revealed by the emergent practices of the seventies and eighties, sticks us somehow with our worldliness and delivers us from what we have learned to call "formalism" and "aestheticism."

I have of course hedged this promise even as I have described it. Some part of my hesitation turns on the difficulties of making out the actual weight of "aestheticism," and on the relation of the critique of aestheticism to the sublime, and thus feeds back into the first part of this paper. For the moment, however, I want to pause over some of the underlying difficulties with this general grasp of photography. Most of them hinge upon the casualness with which we think ourselves to understand what is and is not automatic about the work of the camera; most if not all claims about photography as automatic reproduction can be countered by a photographer determined to show his or her art as possessed of all the possibilities and aesthetic flexibility of the medium claimed by, say, a painter. It is difficult to show at this level of argument how as a tool the camera is any different from a painter's brush and palette, and I think it is wrong to try to make this position out.

The problem is that it is often hard to separate this line of argument from another that does, I think, matter. There are two points that seem to me crucial in thinking about photography. The first is usefully displayed as a certain dissymmetry between a commonplace of aesthetic argument and its photographic equivalent. The commonplace is the question of the accidental work of art—monkeys who produce *Hamlet*, waves whose retreat leaves the sand rippled so as to look like the text of the "Intimations" ode, the chimp who "paints" a Vermeer. I am not interested in settling the question of the status of such works, but only in the difficulty of making this commonplace count for photography. The chimp who takes a picture does not present the same conundrum as his possibly-painterly counterpart; there is no real problem about saying the chimp took a picture. This is a way of registering what *is* automatic about photography, and it comes out as a certain indubitability of its production (not of the truth of that production, just its fact). The point is not quite that the photograph is indexical rather than iconic, but that it interferes with that distinction: to take a picture is to make a picture.

The second point is just that the camera is a linear perspective machine, designed to produce linear perspective renditions of the world. Its products have a peculiar ability to show us something about the fate of the world so realized; it can conduct a critique of vision that can be conducted nowhere else. To put it another way, closer to the terms of the first part of this paper, it can show us something about the mutual implication of presentation and representation.[11] As Rosalind Krauss nicely puts it, "what the camera frames, and thereby makes visible, is the automatic writing of the world: the constant, uninterrupted production of signs."[12] It is frequently tempting to turn this into a formulation to the effect that the photograph shows us the socially constituted nature of the real—and this is not false unless we start surreptitiously reading this social constitution or construction as a figure for an imposition upon or deprivation of "the really real." This move reinstates the radical distinction of presentation and representation that is the target of Heideggerean and Derridean critique, and shifts toward a different sense of "critique of representation" which would find in representation itself an index and agent of oppression.[13] And this is, in the end, to fall back into a kind of modernism (as does the inverse move that would urge the liberation of representation from presentation). In a sense we are back on a different version of the path that led Greenberg from "Avant-Garde and Kitsch" to "Modernist Painting." There is a tendency now to try to retrieve an early Greenberg from the wrong turn represented by this later position; I would argue that there is no "wrong turn" in Greenberg, just an exemplary tale about the fate of one kind of politically informed criticism that it is in some degree our job not to repeat.

The photograph gives us the world as in need of reading, and it does so in the face of our expectation that it will give us the world as sheer fact of vision. This is a demand, and we will call that demand "political" or "ethical," depending to a considerable degree upon our willingness to see the photographic text as registering the fate of presence or its suppression. In the end the illusion of choice here is no doubt false: I am arguing only the necessity of both responses.

If we return to Krauss's formulation we may be struck by the insistence of the word "frames" in her description of what the camera does. What does it mean here? One way of exploring the irrelevance of the accidental work topos to photography would be to suggest that the question the accidental work raises is whether or not it is (deserves to be, intends to be) framed. To ask this is to ask something about the way in which a notion of convention does or does not inform the presumed work—and the irrelevance of this question to the photograph would then point to something natural (and thus "automatic" and unframed or unframable) about photography. But under those circumstances in which the discovery of the camera is of the constant and uninterrupted production of signs, the as it were deep conventionality of the world, this will not do. We would have rather to say that photography demands we think nature and convention as not opposed in this way, but peculiarly conjoined: the camera exposes the naturalness of convention and raises no question of frame because for it there is always already a frame. Photography reinterprets and inverts the temptation offered by institutional theories of art; where they would suggest that an object is art because it is, in effect, framed, photography would suggest that framing is a consequence of our having things at all. One might recall here the peculiar structure of Heidegger's meditation on the Van Gogh, and one might be able now to address the temptation to describe as "cinematic" the movement of his thought into the shoe and out into the world. The discovery of the camera—the discovery Heidegger would attribute to art as such—is then that the world counts as frame or support for these things (if, that is, they count for us at all). In more "formalist" terms one might say that since the photograph has no frame but only an edge, the question of what one might be tempted to call its "deductive structure" is a question of the world that offers itself as the image's support. Here there would be no difference between a formalist and an ethical or political criticism: questions about the formal structure of the image just are questions about its worldliness. It would be a mistake about the nature of the medium to think that a formalist photographic criticism should take the form of a concentration on considerations of composition, frame, and the like.

But it would be equally a mistake to think that the photograph can simply deliver us from formalism, from the question of medium. Rather, it makes unavoidable the prospect of the world itself as a medium (the insight we try and fail to register with the thought that everything is or has become representation). This returns us to everything in Kant that cuts deeper than Greenberg's reduction of the judgment of taste to a matter of the eye, and leaves us in particular once again before that peculiarly disjunctive mediation Kant locates in the experience of sublimity.[14]

There is then a particular passage in the *Third Critique* I am left trying to read, one that has always been somewhat opaque to me: section 59, entitled "Of Beauty as the Symbol of Morality." What is still legible here is perhaps what I want to call "the ethical," and it is certainly not irrelevant to my sense of the stakes in this passage—although it may well be irrelevant to Kant's argument—that the first example Kant produces for his notion of "symbol" is political (the relation between a despotic state and a hand mill); I see this as answering parergonally to the framing political metaphors of the introduction to the book. This exemplary invagination is perhaps just the inverse of the one I hope to produce.[15]

Whatever the section is about it is not, or not simply, beauty. It is, I think, in general true that from section 30 on the beautiful and the sublime are radically entangled with one another in the logic of Kant's text. Certainly the definition of symbol advanced early on ties it to reason and therefore the sublime, and the general discussion of symbol and indirect presentation relates back to earlier discussions of genius and aesthetic attributes that are deeply involved in the rhetoric of sublimity. Perhaps the most interesting bit here is the moment at which Kant poses certain of his own key terms—ground, dependence, substance—as improper, indirect, and merely symbolic. The result here is that we are in effect unable to read Kant's argument (or, to put it another way, we are compelled to read Kant's text). The argument maintains that "in this faculty the judgment does not see itself, as in empirical judging, subjected to a heteronomy of empirical laws; it gives the law to itself in respect of the objects of so pure a satisfaction . . ." and moves on to conclude that "in this supersensible ground, therefore, the theoretical faculty is bound together in unity with the practical in a way, though common, yet unknown,"[16] which would be fine if we could keep ourselves from stumbling over the indirectness and heteronomy of the word "ground" itself. If we do stumble here, then what we will perhaps see is not the longed-for autonomy of law but something more like law as itself the fact of irreducible heteronomy. This would then mark the point at which the ethical insists even as it withdraws from any given or giveable ethics. It insists in and as a problem we can characterize either as a problem of translation or one of representation; in either case it remains only so long as we continue reading, continue writing, prolonging the modern postally. The urge will be, as it was for Greenberg, to deliver ourselves from this system, to let the postmodern stand before us, to name and date it, to call it the time when space counts and we are freed of history, and so on. Much like modernism in Greenberg's hands, postmodernism bids now to become at once a period and an end to periods, one more of the endless ruses of Hegelian reason.

Frederick Jameson, arguing for the postmodern, cites Marx aptly:

> In a well-known passage, Marx powerfully urges us to do the impossible, namely to think this development [capitalism and the deployment of bourgeois culture] positively *and* negatively all at once; to achieve in other words, a type of thinking that would be capable of grasping the demonstrably baleful features of capitalism along with its extraordinary and liberating dynamism simultane-

> ously, within a single thought, and without attenuating any of the force of either judgment. We are, somehow, to lift our minds to a point at which it is possible to understand that capitalism is at one and the same time the best thing that has ever happened to the human race, and the worst. The lapse from this austere dialectical imperative to the more comfortable stance of the taking of moral positions is inveterate and all too human.[17]

What we want to call postmodernism only tightens the vice here. We can no longer be certain that we know the political from what it would contest, no longer know well which of our positionings are comfortable, inveterate, and all too human, and which not. The "austere dialectical imperative" is tangled in its still more austere revision as the thought of the eternal return of the same and the revision that imposes on our imaginations of time and history. Heidegger writes, repeating Marx:

> Where the danger is as the danger, there the saving power is already thriving also. The latter does not appear incidentally. The saving power is not secondary to the danger. The selfsame danger is, when it is *as* the danger, the saving power. The danger is the saving power, inasmuch as it brings the saving power out of its—the danger's—concealed essence that is ever susceptible of turning.[18]

"The Cultural Politics of Postmodernism," in this settlement lies the danger; in the hesitations and turns within its act of nomination lies perhaps something that can be taken as saving—but only as it disturbs the security of that name, resists it in at once its own name and the name of some other. A symposium on the cultural politics of postmodernism may in the end be nothing more than a symposium in modernism unless we can respond to the pressure that makes each of its terms tremble and that we are, I think, still in the process of learning to call "ethical."

Notes

1. See, among others, Jean-Luc Nancy, *L'impératif catégorique* (Paris: Flammarion, 1983) and Robert Bernascni, "Deconstruction and the Possibility of Ethics" in John Sallis, ed., *Deconstruction and Philosophy: The Texts of Jacques Derrida* (Chicago: Univ. of Chicago Press, 1987).

2. On this general topic, see Jacques Derrida, "Sending on: Representation," trans. Peter and Mary Ann Caws, *Social Research* 49, no. 2 (Summer, 1982), as well as Jonathan Arac's chapter "Postmodernism, Politics, and the Impasse of the New York Intellectuals" in his *Critical Genealogies: Historical Situations*

for Postmodern Literary Studies (New York: Columbia University Press, 1987).

3. Martin Heidegger, *The Question Concerning Technology*, trans. William Lovitt (New York: Harper & Row, 1977) 116.

4. Heidegger here seems to me close in certain ways to Benjamin in the "Epistemo-Critical Prologue" to *The Origin of the German Tragic Drama*, trans. John Osborne (London: NLB, 1977).

5. In Martin Heidegger, *Poetry, Language, Thought*, trans. Albert Hofstadter (New York: Harper & Row, 1971).

6. See Jacques Derrida, "Resitutions of the Truth in Painting" in *The Truth in Painting*, trans. Geoff Bennington and Ian McLeod (Chicago: University of Chicago Press, 1987).

7. This oxymoron is a central trope of the sublime whose fate can be followed from Burke through Hegel and Heidegger to Lyotard and Baudrillard, as it weaves together and apart our imaginations of both art and theory.

8. See Paul Guyer, *Kant and the Claims of Taste* (Cambridge: Harvard University Press, 1979).

9. On this topic, see Steven Knapp, *Personification and the Sublime* (Cambridge: Harvard University Press, 1985) as well as the numerous discussions by Paul de Man.

10. It is for me a striking oddity of Jameson's discussions of postmodernism that they emerge through a reflection on architecture.

11. Lacan and Barthes both take up in explicitly photographic terms the more general reflection on the relation between presentation and representation, wound and frame, engaged by Heidegger and Derrida. George Bataille is a central resource for this line of thought.

12. Rosalind Krauss, "Photography in the Service of Surrealism" in Rosalind Krauss and Jane Livingston, *L'Amour fou: Photography and Surrealism* (New York: Abbeville Press, 1985) 35.

13. See, for example, Craig Owens, "The Discourse of Others: Feminists and Postmodernism," in Hal Foster, ed., *The Anti-Aesthetic* (Port Townsend: Bay Press, 1983).

14. It is just here that I would locate the interest of Rosalind Krauss' recent suite of essays working back and forth across the distance between surrealist photography and the theory that arises in its wake. The residual tug of formalism, the uncertainty about the relations between theory and history, the uneasiness about the political import of these things—all this seems to me about right.

15. Nor is it irrelevant that the metaphors which frame the *Third Critique* and assign it its architectonic task are also political; indeed the playing of framing metaphors and framed examples here would be but another version of Heidegger's framing and framed shoes. It is hard to read the sense or weight of Kant's appeal to "architectonics" in general. One is tempted to take it (Kant is tempted to take it) as about things like foundations and keystones, but Kant—unlike Burke—tends to think of architecture as tied to beauty and questions of things framed or framing themselves. Heidegger continues and complicates this reading of architecture in "The Origin of the Work of Art" and elsewhere. I am tempted to say that what survives in Kant and should matter to us is not the talk of foun-

dations but an argument, half-made and half-enacted, about the mutual framing or support of the means through which we have a world—so that a world without art would be a world without politics not because the one is the other but because we never have the world or our activites in it unframed. What I am trying to call "the ethical" would be the insistence of this fact.

16. Immanuel Kant, *Critique of Judgement*, trans. J. H. Bernard (New York: Hafner Press, 1951), section 59.

17. Fredric Jameson, "Postmodernism, or The Cultural Logic of Late Capitalism," *New Left Review* 146 (July-August, 1984): 86.

18. Heidegger, *The Question Concerning Technology*, 42.

Wild Signs: The Breakup of the Sign in '70s Art

HAL FOSTER

IN AN ESSAY A FEW YEARS AGO I POINTED TO TWO BASIC POSITIONS WITHIN POST-modernist art: one aligned with neoconservative politics, the other associated with poststructuralist theory.[1] In all apparent ways, I argued, these practices are diametrically opposed: neoconservative postmodernism proclaims a return not only of historicist figuration (after the supposed amnesia of modernist abstraction) but also of the privileged artist (despite contemporary diagnoses of his [sic] death), while poststructuralist postmodernism produces a critique of just such categories and configurations. Moreover, while neoconservative postmodernism tends merely to counter formalist modernism with a practice of pastiche (the false populism of which covers for an elitist traditionalism), poststructuralist postmodernism works explicitly to exceed, in its various texts, images, films and objects, both formalist aesthetic categories (the disciplinary order of painting, sculpture, etc.) and traditionalist cultural oppositions (high versus mass culture, autonomous versus utilitarian art). Yet, I argued further, what seems diametrically opposed here is in fact dialectically connected, for the pastiche of neoconservative postmodernism does not redeem historical figuration or integral subjectivity any more than the textuality of poststructuralist postmodernism deconstructs them; rather each practice marks the disintegration of both these forms. Whether in the guise of a neoexpressionist painting or a multimedia performance, each practice manifests the process of spectacular reification that is so intensive in late capitalism; in particular, each attests to a fetishistic fragmentation of the sign—which poststructuralist theory often valorizes and postmodernist practice often performs—that is fundamental to the cultural logic of capital.[2]

Yet this short history of the sign remained very speculative and sketchy; here, then, I want to take it up again in relation to certain models of art in the 1970s, for it seems to me that the fragmentation of the sign, if not grasped as such in much art and criticism of the period, is nonetheless structural to them, so much so that for it *not* to become evident required a certain disavowal. So, too, I want to suggest that related poststructuralist theories of the time—especially ones that reject the concept of totality—also make internal this capitalist logic of reification and fragmentation, and ironically nowhere more so than when they presume to be most postmarxist. Of course, such a symptomatic reading of art and theory runs the risk, often associated with Lukàcs, of a reduction of cultural practice to a mere reflection of socio-economic forces. Here, however, my premise is the more proper Marxian recognition that theory is only as developed as its object (in this case, art) and that both are caught up in the contradictions of the moment in which they are formed—in short, that cultural categories, including concepts of the sign, possess a historicity that it is the task of criticism to apprehend.

Autonomy and Textuality

But how exactly does one historicize the (post)modern sign? Several genealogies can be contrived, and I want to pose a few here, partly in order to reinscribe them later in relation to art of the '70s. The first two, one well known, the other less so, derive from signal poststructuralist texts of Derrida ("Structure, Sign and Play in the Human Sciences," 1966) and Barthes (*S/Z*, 1970). I select these (rather than, say, the Foucauldean typology of the sign in *The Order of Things*) not only because they implicitly historicize the sign in relation to two specific shifts, one associated with market capitalism, the other with high modernism, but also because as they do so they reveal certain preconditions of the poststructuralist moment.

In *S/Z* Barthes is on the lookout for slippages (linguistic, narrative, sexual, psychological, social, political) in the symbolic order of the world of the 1830 Balzac story "Sarrazine"—slippages prompted by the enigmatic (non)center of the text, the castrato Zambinella, "a figure in a complicated relation to the phallus,"[3] to say the least. Early in the story

Balzac laments, vis-à-vis the mysterious keepers of the opera singer, the new social system of bourgeois money: "no one asks to see your family tree because everyone knows how much it cost." Barthes in turn theorizes this passage from the old feudal regime of hierarchical origins—of fixed wealth (land, gold)—to the new bourgeois regime of equivalent signs—of promiscuous paper money—as a shift from the order of the index to that of the sign:

> The difference between feudal society and bourgeois society, index and sign, is this: the index has an origin, the sign does not: to shift from index to sign is to abolish the last (or first) limit, the origin, the basis, the prop, to enter into the limitless process of equivalences, representations that nothing will ever stop, orient, fix, sanction . . . the signs (monetary, sexual) are wild because . . . the two elements *interchange*, signified and signifier revolving in an endless process: what is bought can be sold, the signified can become signifier, and so on.[4]

Yet this historicization of the sign in relation to the cultural order of market capitalism—"an order of representation" that will soon prompt the first modern art—is conceived in terms far more appropriate to the cultural order of *late* capitalism—"a limitless process of equivalences." No doubt this condition of "wild signs" is emergent in the moment witnessed by Balzac, but it is not dominant until our own moment (which is, after all, often described as one of spectacular simulacra)—until, that is, the conjuncture from which Barthes writes 140 years after Balzac. Here then Barthes projects elements of a contemporary political and libidinal economy onto its beginnings, which suggests that the shift from the order of the index to that of the sign is completed (or rather repeated to the point where it is grasped as such) only in the present of his own text, that is, in the '70s. And such a shift does in fact govern salient aspects of the art of the period.

Derrida also projects a poststructuralist concept of the sign onto history, yet, unlike Barthes, he does so not in relation to the linguistic order of market capitalism (i.e., of early modernism) but implicitly in relation to the linguistic order of high modernism (i.e., of monopoly capitalism). In "Structure, Sign and Play in the Discourse of Human Sciences" (1966), his famous deconstruction of Lévi-Straussean anthropology, Derrida writes of a "rupture" at which point it became necessary to think the concept of structure outside the concept of a fixed center or presence:

> This was the moment when language invaded the universal problematic, the moment when, in the absence of a center or origin, everything became discourse— . . . that is to say, a system in which the central signified, the original or transcendental signified, is never absolutely present outside a system of differences. The absence of the transcendental signified extends the domain and the play of signification infinitely.[5]

Pressed to specify this decentering, Derrida alludes to the Nietzschean critique of truth, the Freudian critique of self-presence and the Heideggerean critique of metaphysics; yet it is surely the Saussurean concept of the diacritical sign that most directly allows this new "play of signification." In any case, all these references allow us to identify the rupture remarked by Derrida—in structure, language, representation—as the rupture of modernism; and the epistemic connection between structural linguistics and modernist art is clear. ("The extraordinary contribution of [cubist] collage," Rosalind Krauss has written, "is that it is the first instance within the pictorial arts of anything like a systematic exploration of the conditions of representability entailed by the sign."[6]) Significantly, however, Derrida refuses to locate this decentering historically: "It is no doubt part of the totality of an era, our own," he states enigmatically, "but still it has always already begun to proclaim itself. . . ." Could it be that he here intimates the preconditions of his own recognition: that this decentering is only grasped as such—is only *lived* as such—in his own poststructuralist present? As with Barthes's "limitless process of equivalences," so with Derrida's infinite "play of signification": though surely related archeologically to the ruptures of market capitalism (Barthes) and high modernism (Derrida), they are only "achieved" in our late-capitalist, postmodernist moment, of which poststructuralism is a symptomatic discourse, one that comprehends earlier ruptures in the sign only because it reflects yet another rupture which it *cannot* comprehend for the simple reason that it participates in it.[7]

Two related genealogies of the sign may clarify this symptomatic aspect of poststructuralism. For both Jean Baudrillard and Fredric Jameson, (post)structuralism narrates a process of progressive abstraction, first of the referent (as announced by structural linguistics) and then of the signified (whereby in poststructuralism every signified becomes another signifier). This process is easy enough to relate to the dynamic of (post)modernism: abstraction of the referent in high modernism (e.g., cubism) and of the signified in postmodernism (e.g., again, our world of simulacral images [Baudrillard] or schizophrenic signifiers [Jameson]). For both critics the ultimate agent of this abstraction is capital: "For finally it was capital which was the first to feed throughout its history on the destruction of every referent . . . in order to establish its radical law of equivalence and exchange."[8] In this way an important historical relationship is suggested among the different stages of (post)structuralism, (post)modernism and capital, whereby the former function as cultural codes—critical and collusive—of the latter. Indeed, not only does the diacritical logic of the structuralist sign (of signifier and signified) replicate the diacritical logic of the commodity (of use value and exchange value), as Baudrillard suggests, but so too may the poststructuralist critique of the sign promote the very "fetishism of the signifier" that is fundamental to the ideological code of late capitalism.[9] Jameson historicizes the same dynamic in terms of reification:

> in a first moment [i.e., of structural linguistics, of modernism], reification "liberated" the sign from its referent, but this is not a force to be released with impunity. Now, in a second moment [i.e., of poststructuralism, of postmodernism], it continues its work of dissolution, penetrating the interior of the sign itself and liberating the signifier from the signified, or from meaning proper. This play, no longer of a realm of signs, but of pure or literal signifiers freed from the ballast of their signifieds, their former meanings, now generates a new kind of textuality in all the arts.[10]

Below I want to test this model of a "new kind of textuality in all the arts" in relation to recent art theory, but first its aggressive historicism must be tempered, for the abstraction of the artistic sign does not proceed so evenly—there are repressions, repetitions and resistances to factor in. Now one logic of modernism is, indeed, to bracket the referent, first in order to approach an autonomy of the sign (as, say, in Cézanne), then to explore its arbitrariness (analytically in Cubism, anarchically in Dadaism); but this modernist "liberation" of the sign does not lead directly to a postmodernist "play" of signifiers. In the postwar reinvention of the avant-garde, modernist autonomy (or, in the language of Clement Greenberg, self-referential purity) is reestablished as the criterion of art—precisely *against* any (dadaist) arbitrariness of the sign. And yet, after abstract expressionism, this very arbitrariness is in turn reestablished, especially with figures like Robert Rauschenberg and Jasper Johns. In fact, with Johns the arbitrariness of the sign is pushed to the point of the dissolution remarked by Jameson—to the point, that is, where signifiers (in Johns letters, numbers, color names, etc.) do become literal, "freed from the ballast of their signified."

But this incipient textuality is also in turn countered with minimalism, a contemporary of structuralism that in its obsession with "objecthood" apparently achieves the autonomy of the artistic sign demanded by the dominant logic of modernism . . . only to see this autonomy dispersed across an "expanded field" of art that is again textual in nature (Pop art, photorealist art, conceptual art, process art, body art, diaristic art, performance art, earth and site-specific art, video art, institution-critical art, feminist art . . .).[11] In fact, this dialectic—between a minimalistic autonomy of the artistic sign and its textual dispersal across new forms and/or its Pop collapse into mass-cultural ones—is operative throughout '60s culture (for example, in avant-garde cinema between the structurally autonomous films of Michael Snow on the one hand and the disruptively textual films of Godard on the other).[12] However, in the late '60s and early '70s, the textual term of this dialectic comes to dominate, and the question is how does this textualist transformation occur?

Let me begin with a test case. Frank Stella is an exemplary painter of late modernism, a principal proponent of autonomy (or, again, self-referentiality). His early mature work (ca. 1959–65) is mostly based on fundamental forms such as crosses and stars whereby depicted design and actual support are (nearly) coincident. In this work Stella is concerned to (re)ground the structure of painting as firmly as possible in the stability of simple signs.[13] That he does so, however, under the pressure of the historical *in*stability of the sign is suggested by his later work. For example, in his "Protractor" paintings design and support are at once so coterminous and so conflictual that the pictorial sign is held together even as its fundamental *dis*unity is exposed. By the mid '70s his work is given over more and more to this instability. Indeed, Stella exacerbates it: he first fetishizes particular signs of modernist painting (e.g., constructivism) and then simulates whole codes of historical painting—to the point in the '80s where one might find signifiers of linear perspective, of the three grounds of landscape painting, and of the modernist grid all ajumble in one construction. In short, the progression of his art from simple signs to fragmentary signifiers participates in the very negation of form, bespeaks the very dissolution of the sign, associated with the abstractive process of (post)modern capital. This negation is as transformative as it is decorative, as critical as it is replicative.

And it is hardly unique: this process is operative throughout different art forms of the late '60s and early '70s; in fact, it may be this alone that connects them. Faced with the dissolution of the artistic sign, some artists sought to reground it—first fetishistically in various new materials and processes (as in minimalism, process art, "postminimalism"), then literally in the presence of the body, of the site, of actual space-time (as in body art, site- specific art, performance); while other artists underscored this dissolution—either demonstrated the reification of artistic language (as in much conceptual art) or enacted its material fragmentation (as in the many ephemeral installations of the period). Often presented as resistant to the commodity status of the art object, these strategies seem in retrospect to partake, indirectly at least, in the very fetishism of the signifier that, again for Baudrillard, is part and parcel of our consumerist "passion for the code."

In any case, few artists grasped the disintegrative dynamic of the sign at this time. (There are exceptions: certainly Robert Smithson reflected, particularly in his textual site/nonsite works, on the concept of a structure outside the concept of a center.) In fact, this dynamic was not adequately critiqued until the institution-critical art and the psychoanalytical-feminist art that came to the fore in the United States only in the mid and late '70s. Contemporaneous with the Althusserian and Foucauldean critiques of ideological state apparatuses, institution-critical art implicitly rejected the position of an infinite "play of signification" in favor of an investigation of its institutional affiliations with power, while feminist art explicitly deconstructed "the tyranny of the [phallic] signifier"[14] in favor of nonsexist forms of cultural production and reception. But again, in the early '70s, these aspects of the artistic sign were not yet foregrounded in art. Indeed, the terms necessary for such an understanding were only established in American art theory near the end of the decade—and then not entirely consciously, for the two texts that I have in mind are silent on the historical forces that determine the very fragmentation of the artistic sign which they otherwise narrate.

Indices and Allegories

In "Notes on the Index: Seventies Art in America" (1977), Rosalind Krauss seeks a principle that might order the pluralistic art of the decade, and she finds it not in the art-historical category of style but in the semiotic order of the index. "As distinct from symbols," she writes, "indexes [e.g., footprints] establish their meaning along the axis of a physical relationship to their referents."[15] Right away this model refocuses such characteristic art of the '70s as body or installation art—as an indexical regrounding of art in presence subsequent to an erosion of representation.[16] Yet, Krauss argues, this shift to the indexical also occurred over 50 years before with Duchamp who, after the cubist abstraction of the referent, confronted the arbitrariness of the sign: "It was as if Cubism forced for Duchamp the issue of whether pictorial language could continue to signify directly, could picture anything like an accessible set of contents" [p. 202]. Indeed, not only did Duchamp *foreground* the instability of the sign (e.g., in the metonymic confusions of the homonymous phrases scribbled on his "optical machines," in the sexual confusions of his alter-ego Rrose Selavy), but he also *regrounded* the sign in indexical marks (of which, as Krauss notes, the painting *Tu M'* (1918) is a virtual catalogue, replete with shadow images of the readymades, a play of linguistic shifters in the title and even a representation of an index finger). According to Krauss, these indexical operations govern all the work of Duchamp, whether photographic (she reads *The Large Glass* "as a kind of photograph") or readymade, since the photograph as a "sub- or pre-symbolic" trace is inherently indexical and the readymade is "a sign which is inherently 'empty,' its signification a function of only this one instance, guaranteed by the existential presence of just this object" [p. 206].

In the second part of her essay, Krauss relates these Duchampian strategies to '70s art; and in fact the "trauma of signification" that prompted the one recurs to prompt the other: on the one hand, an abstraction of the sign—first in cubism, then in minimalism—and, on the other, a predominance of the photographic—first in the mass culture faced by Duchamp, then in the consumer culture embraced by Pop. (The Duchampian strategies of '70s art also fit neatly in the Duchampian genealogy of the last 25 years—midway between the '60s recovery of the readymade in minimalism and Pop and its '80s elaboration in appropriation art.) Here Krauss again relates the indexical to the photographic, the structure of which she defines first as a "reduction of the conventional sign to a trace" and then, after Barthes, as a "message without a code" [p. 211]. Now one purpose of this connection between the indexical and the photographic is to order the diverse forms of '70s art under a single principle—"the registration of sheer physical presence"—whether this be indexical as in installation art or photographic as in video. But the more important purpose is to grasp the logic of this "presence" as a substitute for a "language of aesthetic conventions" [p. 209] that breaks down in the '70s as it had at the moment of Duchamp. In short, according to Krauss, '70s art also faces a "tremendous arbitrariness with regard to meaning," and its primary response is to resort to "the mute presence of an uncoded event" [p. 212].

This is a brilliant account of much '70s art, but its insight into structural logic makes for a partial blindness regarding historical process.[17] The very premises of the indexical model of '70s art – that artistic signs can be "empty," that cultural messages can exist "without a code" – are disproven by later artists involved in a critique of (art) institutions and representations: for these artists, no body or site, representation or event, is ever simply present or uncoded. Indeed, some artists (e.g., Michael Asher, Hans Haacke) who elaborated on indexical art in the '70s came to treat site-specificity not phenomenologically in terms of mute presence but discursively in terms of institutional power. So too other artists (e.g., Martha Rosler, Sherrie Levine) who elaborated on photographic art of the '70s came to treat the documentary status of photography not as a message without a code to explore but as an ideological function to critique. In fact, just as the first artists would conclude that, far from uncoded, (institutional) sites actually overcode art, so too the second would conclude that, far from uncoded (photographic) representations are actually texts that may project an effect of the real but do so only according to the logic of simulacral myth.[18] Of course, Krauss is hardly responsible for the limitations of her object; on the contrary, she outlines its logic so clearly that its historical process may now stand revealed: the shift to the indexical in '70s art – the substitution of simple marks of presence for an eroded referent and an erratic signified – is a response to the progressive dissolution of the late-modernist sign; and this dissolution reflects the penetration of the artistic sign by the capitalist dynamic of reification and fragmentation. Such is the political unconscious of this semiotic breakdown, which, precisely because it was unconscious, could not then be grasped in its historical agency.

This rewriting must now be tested against the other major model of '70s art – that such art refuses the late-modernist paradigm of symbolic totality in favor of a new postmodernist paradigm of allegorical textuality. Posed primarily by Craig Owens, this model can be decoded as a response to the next stage of this dissolution of the artistic sign: from its indexical regrounding in presence (body or site) to its allegorical dispersal as a play of signifiers (text). And yet this theory of an "allegorical impulse" in art is also blind to the capitalist dynamic which governs its object: like the indexical model, it brilliantly theorizes art in terms of internal transformations of the sign, but it too elides the historical preconditions both of these aesthetic transformations and of its own theoretic construction.

If the subject of "Notes on the Index" is the erosion of the conventional pictorial sign, the subject of "Earthwords" (1979), a review-essay of *The Writings of Robert Smithson,* is the transgression of entire aesthetic categories.[19] In this early text Owens links postmodernism (in the figure of Smithson) with poststructuralism (in the figure of Derrida) by means of the decentering operative in both practices: it is, he argues, the eruption of language at the center of '60s and '70s art (e.g., conceptual art, artist writings, diaristic art, textual modes of documentation) that dislocates the visual order of modernism and prepares the textual space of postmodernism. Forget that for Foucault it is this eruption that initiates the modern, not the postmodern, episteme; the important connection here is the one implied between poststructuralist decentering in language and postmodernist fragmentation in art. In "The Allegorical Impulse" (1980) Owens thinks this relationship in terms of the Benjaminian concept of allegory: postmodernist art is allegorical not simply in its stress on the ruinous and the fragmentary, on immanent spaces (e.g., ephemeral site-specific work) and contingent forms (e.g., enigmatic images appropriated from the media), but more importantly in its impulse to dedefine verbal and visual categories, to disarrange stylistic norms, to transgress modernist boundaries, to exploit the gap between signifier and signified. Owens cites these practices in particular: "appropriation, site-specificity, impermanence, accumulation, discursivity, hybridization."[20]

But, as is now clear, there are problems with this model, both definitional and strategic. On the first count, one cannot strictly oppose an allegorical postmodernist paradigm to a symbolic modernist one, for each impulse—the utopian, transcendental, totalistic *and* the fallen, immanent, contingent—is not only dialectically necessary to the other but is so actively within modernism. In fact, as Owens works out his genealogy of the allegorical impulse, he finds it, via Benjamin and Baudelaire "at the origin of *modernism*. . . ."[21] On the second count, his use of Benjaminian allegory tends to be formalist in its very anti-formalism; that is, in this early essay Owens is concerned primarily with the rhetorical ways in which the allegorical mode disrupts the formal autonomy of modernist art. At this point the stake of postmodernism is aesthetic—the replacement of one (symbolic) mode by another (allegorical) one—or, best, avant-garde—allegorical art is valued because it transgresses formalist categories. Analysis of the economic processes and political ramifications of postmodernism is not yet developed. Thus, for example, though Owens speaks incisively of reification of language in Smithson, of history as dissolution and decay in Benjamin, of verbal and visual forms destructured in postmodernist art, he does not reflect on the greater forces that govern these deconstructions—other than to suggest that it is the impulse of this artist or that theorist. (The word "capital" does not appear once—an extrordinary fact in an essay largely based on the Benjaminian concept of the allegorical in modern culture.)

In fairness, this apolitical reading of allegory was characteristic of the American reception of Benjamin in the '70s: his concept of allegory, received in terms of *The Origin of German Tragic Drama* rather than the Baudelaire writings and sifted through Derrida and de Man, was depoliticized; and his movement towards Marxism was reversed. In his more recent work Owens has in turn reversed this reversal; nevertheless, in "The Allegorical Impulse" he too rewrites Benjaminian allegory in terms of Derridean textuality and de Manian illegibility. But these characteristics of postmodernist art are complex symptoms, not transparent explanations: though they do, indeed, point to an "erosion of meaning" [p. 216], this erosion must finally be referred not to the theoretical apparatus of allegory, but again to the historical process of capitalist reification and fragmentation. At the conclusion of his essay Owens narrates the (post)modernist abstraction of the sign outlined above:

> Modernist theory presupposes that mimesis, the adequation of an image to a referent, can be bracketed or suspended, and that the art object itself can be substituted (metaphorically) for its referent. . . . For reasons that are beyond the scope of this essay, this fiction has become increasingly difficult to maintain. Postmodernism neither brackets nor suspends the referent but works to problematize the activity of reference [p. 235].

Significantly, this narration of the abstractive process stops short of its historical reasons, which remain precisely beyond the scope of this particular poststructuralist model. And yet if explored these reasons might in turn problematize the role of postmodernist art in this problematization of reference—as symptom rather than agent—perhaps along lines suggested long ago by Benjamin: "The devaluation of the world of objects in allegory is outdone within the world of objects itself by the commodity."[22]

Allegories and Commodities

Like "Notes on the Index," "Allegorical Impulse" is hardly responsible for the conceptual limitations of its moment. In the late '70s the fragmentation of postmodernist art almost had to be thought in terms of an allegorical play of signifiers, in part because neither the discursive analysis of the artistic sign in institutional-critical art nor the psychoanalytical critique of its phallocentric subject in feminist art were as yet received in the United States. Feminist art was a particular blind spot—the conjuncture that prompted it in Britain, a nexus of feminist criticism and Althusser, film theory and Lacan, had not fully developed here. However, a reading of institution-critical art had emerged by 1980; significantly, it too applied the Benjaminian concept of allegory but in its Marxian formulation—of the allegorical as a critical mode of aesthetic practice in the culture of the commodity. Presented primarily by Benjamin Buchloh, this reading regarded the allegorical less in Derridean terms of textuality than in Barthesian terms of myth or ideology critique. Buchloh noted strategies similar to Owens—"appropriation and depletion of meaning, fragmentation and dialectical juxtaposition of fragments, and separation of signifier and signified"[23]—but he positioned them differently: not only in a genealogy of institution-critical art (from Duchamp through Pop and Marcel Broodthaers to Dara Birnbaum and others) but also as dialectical responses to the montaged sensorium of (post)modern life. In this way Buchloh returned recent allegorical art not only to its archaeological beginnings in capitalist technique but also to its historical subject: reification.

But problems have arisen with this allegorical practice too. One such problem, noted by both Buchloh and Owens, is its rapport with a melancholic posture—a posture of political passivity before a social world so reified as to appear inert, the history of which is then regarded almost posthistorically as so many ruinous *tableaux vivants* for aesthetic contemplation. Thus, art that was deemed allegorical (e.g., Robert Longo, Jack Goldstein, Troy Brauntuch) is in fact melancholic: its concern is the enigma of the historical or the opacity of the significant more than the critical redemption of lost moments or appropriated meanings. Such art is also spectacular: it is seduced to the point of replication by the late-capitalist transformation of events, objects, even people into so many images to consume. (Indeed, its "allegorical" aspects—an aesthetic contemplation of the historical, a rhetorical confusion of the temporal and spatial—"were discussed in 1928 by Georg Lukàcs as the essential features of the collective condition of reification" [p. 56], a condition which late-capitalist spectacle merely elaborates upon.) With this aesthetic of spectacle, such art has inaugurated a new moment or model for art of the present: call it, after the indexical paradigm and the allegorical impulse, a conventionalist model whereby even the most materialist practices (e.g., the Duchampian readymade, analytical abstraction) become so many ahistorical conventions to be consumed, so many detached signifiers to be manipulated. Not restricted to any one style, this conventionalist art rehabilitates lost referents, only to reproduce them as simulacra: in so doing it does not contest our political economy of the sign but rather plays right to its market machinations. In fact, this art extends—to a degree that seems almost conscious—the fetishistic fragmentation of the artistic sign under discussion here.[24]

Buchloh is aware of the dangers of such a collapse; nevertheless, he insists on the potential criticality of allegorical art. Rather than rehearse the fetishism-effect of commodification (as conventionalist work does), such art can take this process apart as its own critical procedure:

> The allegorical mind sides with the object and protests against its devaluation to the status of a commodity by devaluating it a second time in allegorical practice. In the splintering of signifier and signified, the allegorist subjects the sign to the same division of functions that the object has undergone in its transformation into a commodity. The repetition of the original act of depletion and the new attribution of meaning redeems the object [p. 44].

Here, as he later acknowledges, Buchloh is very close to the Barthes of *Mythologies* (1957) wherein Barthes argues that the dominant culture operates by appropriation: it abstracts the specific signs of social groups into mere signifiers that are then recorded as general cultural myths (consider, for example, the trajectory of rap music or graffiti art). Against this appropriation Barthes proposed counterappropriation:

> Truth to tell, the best weapon against myth is perhaps to mythify it in its turn, and to produce an *artificial myth:* and this reconstituted myth will in fact be a mythology. . . . All that is needed is to use it as a departure point for a third semiological chain, to take its signification as the first term of a second myth.[25]

This myth-robbery is the allegorical procedure of much appropriation art of the late '70s and early '80s (e.g., Barbara Kruger, Sherrie Levine, Louise Lawler): to break apart the mythical sign, to reinscribe it in a countermythical system and to recirculate it in the distribution form of the commodity-image.

And yet there are potential problems here as well. The issue is not strictly recuperation: that appropriation is now a museum category or that montage is now an "abused gadget . . . for sale." Rather it concerns strategy: when is appropriation a counterappropriation and not a replication? When does montage recode rather than rehearse the dissolution of the sign by capital? By 1970 Barthes had revised his project of myth critique: it presumed too much—a position of scientific truth; besides, it had become part of the doxa. Today, he argued, one must do more—shake the sign, challenge the symbolic.[26] Given the phallocracy of the symbolic, this means one thing in feminist practice: a critical attention regarding positionality in representation. However, in the pervasive conventionalist practice of the present, it means quite another thing: not a critique of the mythical sign, but a fetishistic manipulation of its shattered signifiers. In conventionalist art "the commodity has taken the place of the allegorical way of seeing"[27] once again.

If allegorical counterappropriation is to be critical and not conventionalist, then it must be practiced with social groups that are appropriated and/or excluded in the first place; this includes not only the appropriated others of present society (e.g., indigenous cultures still subject to primitivist abstractions, Afro-American cultures ever pillaged by style industries) but also the excluded others of institutional history (e.g., popular cultures not acknowledged in art museums, proletarian cultures not transmitted in official traditions).[28] To be most effective, critical counterappropriation must take up both these contemporary and historical agendas: it must be performed collectively with appropriated social groups in the present (collectively because these groups are in no need of salvage: they have vital traditions and resistant strategies of their own) and redemptively for such excluded groups in the past (redemptively because, as Benjamin famously remarked, not even the dead—not *especially* the dead—are safe from the history written by the victors). In this way one must not only dislocate cultural signs from myth but also reground them in the social world of everyday experience. It is true that such a practice might presuppose an idealism of the referent—as if the use value of a sign, once abstracted, can be so restored. It is also true that it might presuppose an idealism of the social—that by sheer will artists can become collective producers rather than isolated practitioners. But this hardly makes such a practice utopian: it simply shows that it is not only in cultural production but also in its social field that artistic and critical interventions must now and ever be made.

Notes

1. See my "(Post)Modern Polemics," *New German Critique* 33 (Fall 1984), reprinted in *Recodings: Art, Spectacle, Cultural Politics* (Seattle: Bay Press, 1985).

2. See Fredric Jameson, "Periodizing The 60s," in *The 60s Without Apology*, ed. S. Sayres, A. Stephanson et al. Minneapolis: University of Minnesota Press, 1984) 194- 201.

3. Dana Polan, "Brief Encounters: Mass Culture and the Evacuation of Sense," in *Studies in Entertainment*, ed. Tania Modleski (Bloomington: Indiana University Press, 1986) 173. I am indebted for the Barthes reference to this provocative essay.

4. Roland Barthes, *S/7* (New York: Hill and Wang, 1974) 40.

5. Jacques Derrida, in *Writing and Difference*, trans. Alan Bass (Chicago: University of Chicago Press, 1978) 280.

6. Rosalind Krauss, *The Originality of the Avant-Garde and Other Modernist Myths* (Cambridge: MIT Press, 1984) 34.

7. Often an argument takes on a logic that pushes certain points to the margins; so it is here. Let me simply note two lost tangents.

The shift from the order of the index to that of the sign as outlined by Barthes suggests another passage (outlined by Dana Polan with reference to Jean-Joseph Goux)—a partial, problematic shift in the economy of the subject from the classical capitalist regime of repression meted out by the phallic power of the father to the late-capitalist regime of investment in which the flow of desire is actively incited. Now if we relate this putative shift to the discourse of postmodernism, we can begin to demystify its pervasive ideologeme of *loss* (loss of social narratives, political legitimation, artistic mastery, etc., etc.). For the postmodern sense of loss is registered as such only by various authorities of patriarchy: it is hardly felt by feminists. Nor does this shift mark a loss in any real sense: in practical terms of power it is but a slight reformation of social regime, a partial redeployment of productive bodies. Or as Polan writes: "Power doesn't always take shape as the power of the Symbolic Father, and the overthrow of a centered, authoritative Symbolic may simply mean that other forms of power—relations—often more subtle than the model of a feudal power focused on a lordly figure—have come into dominance. Thus, for Goux, the overthrow of the Law of the Father in the overthrow of gold not only brings about the emergence of a free-floating economic sign, but also ties this emergence to the parallel emergence of a new law that finds its force in the transnational monopoly—the new corporation whose micropolitical channels of control are so widespread and dispersed that no single authoritative father-figure is necessary to put the machine into operation" [pp. 177- 78].

This shift—in the order of subjectivity, in the order of power—is related to the shift remarked by Derrida: from a concept of centered structure to the concept of a "system of difference." As Derrida implies, this rupture, which finds its expression in high modernism and its precondition in monopoly capitalism, is still with us, as indeed monopoly capitalism is still with us, now lifted to a new level of totality in late capitalism. Could it be that the ultimate referent of his "system of differences" is the system of late capitalism—a centerless system which, if not global as a regime, is nonetheless total as a differential order that governs relations throughout the world market? In this system, with its multinational deployment of capital and its international division of labor, center and periphery are indeed destructured; and yet, even as difference is thereby released, it is also continually recaptured and redeployed.

Of course, developments on two such different levels—in deconstructive theory and in late capitalism—cannot be related by mere analogy. Nonetheless, the "field" posited by poststructuralism and postmodernism in the '70s and the "field" constructed by late capitalism for the contemporary subject are somehow related, and this relationship may be mediated, in a partial way, by the reification and fragmentation of the sign. This penetration is not metaphorical; in art it becomes actual in the '60s when, with minimalism and Pop, serial production is made consistently integral to the actual technical production of the work of art. But it is only in the '70s that this penetration of the artistic sign by capital begins to be thought, in however displaced a form.

8. Jean Baudrillard, "The Precession of Simulacre," *Art & Text* 11 (Spring 1983): 28.

9. Baudrillard, *For A Critique of the Political Economy of the Sign*, trans. Charles Levin (St. Louis: Telos Press, 1981) 92.

10. Jameson, 200.

11. For a gloss on these terms, the first associated with Michael Fried, the second with Rosalind Krauss, see my "The Crux of Minimalism," in *Individuals: A Selected History of Contemporary Art* (New York and Los Angeles: Abbeville Press/Los Angeles Museum of Contemporary Art, 1986) 162–83.

12. See Annette Michelson, "Film and The Radical Aspiration," in *Film Theory and Criticism*, ed. G. Mast and M. Cohen (New York: Oxford University Press, 1974) 469–87.

13. ". . . the logic of the deductive structure is . . . shown to be inseparable from the logic of the sign." Krauss, "Sense and Sensibility: Reflections on Post '60s Sculpture," *Artforum* 12, 3 (November 1973): 47.

14. Craig Owens, "The Discourse of Others: Feminists and Postmodernism," in *The Anti-Aesthetics: Essays on Postmodern Culture*, ed. Hal Foster (Seattle: Bay Press, 1983) 59.

15. Krauss, *Originality*, 198. Other page references for this essay are given in the text.

16. A crucial aspect of this subversion of the representational paradigm (and, for that matter, of the abstract paradigm) is the release of the simulacrum into art of the '60s (most obviously in Pop). In fact, it can be argued that modernist abstraction poses no *fundamental* break with the representational paradigm, for the simple reason that it preserves this paradigm in opposition, in cancellation. Such a break must await the simulacral illogic and serial repetition of postmodernist art, which works to erode referential logic on its own terms. Clearly, any avant-gardist celebration of this "subversion" is problematic. For more on this see "The Crux of Minimalism," 178–80.

17. In fairness, this is her stated interest: "I am not so much concerned here with the genesis of this condition within the arts, its historical process, as I am with its internal structure as one now confronts it in a variety of work" (p. 210).

18. For a different reading of the photographic derealization of the image, see Douglas Crimp, "The Photographic Activity of Postmodernism," *October* 15 (Winter 1980): 91–101. Although Crimp conceives the problematic of presence

in '70s art differently than I do here (see his early essay "Pictures"), his reading has been generative.

19. Owens, "Earthwords," *October* 10 (Fall 1979): 120–30.

20. Owens, "The Allegorical Impulse: Toward a Theory of Postmodernism," in *Art After Modernism: Rethinking Representation*, ed. Brian Wallis (Boston and New York: David R. Godine/New Museum of Contemporary Art, 1984) 209. Other page references for this essay are given in the text.

21. Ibid., p. 212. A similar criticism is made (too strongly) by Thomas Crow in "Modernism and Mass Culture in the Visual Arts," in *Modernism and Modernity*, ed. B. Buchloh, S. Guilbault and D. Solkin (Halifax: Nova Scotia Press, 1983) 257. Also see Michael Newman, "Revising Modernism, Representing Postmodernism: Critical Discourses of the Visual Arts," in *Postmodernism*, ICA Documents 5 (London: Institute of Contemporary Arts, 1986) 42–45.

22. Walter Benjamin, "Central Park" (1939) in *New German Critique* 34 (Winter 1985): 34.

23. Benjamin H. D. Buchloh, "Allegorical Procedures: Appropriation and Montage in Contemporary Art," *Artforum*, 21 (September 1982): 44. Other page references for this essay are given in the text.

24. Conventionalist art assumes the avant-gardist recognition par excellence—that art is a matter of historical conventions—but it does not act on the radical possibility of this recognition; i.e., it makes no attempt to return art to social use. Quite the opposite: it surrenders art to the vicious circle of consumerist irrelevance; and it does so by default—it has no collectivity to engage. For more on these "spectacular" and "conventionalist" tendencies, see *Recodings*, 78–97, and my "Signs Taken for Wonders," *Art in America* (June 1986).

25. Roland Barthes, *Mythologies* (New York: Hill & Wang, 1972) 135. Also see *Recodings*, 166–79.

26. Barthes, "Change the Object Itself," in *Image—Music—Text*, trans. Stephen Heath (New York: Hill & Wang, 1977).

27. Benjamin, 52.

28. Jürgen Habermas gives an example of such counterappropriation: "a group of politically motivated, knowledge-hungry workers in 1937 in Berlin . . . who, through an evening high-school education, acquired the intellectual means to fathom the general and social history of European art. Out of the resilient edifice of this objective mind, embodied in works of art which they saw again and again in the museums of Berlin, they started removing their own chips of stone, which they gathered together and reassembled in the context of their own milieu. This milieu was far removed from that of traditional education as well as from the then existing regime. These young workers went back and forth between the edifice of European art and their own milieu until they were able to illuminate both." (Habermas, "Modernity—An Incomplete Project," in *The Anti-Aesthetic*, 13.) The example is not only abstract but also fictional—drawn from *The Aesthetics of Resistance* by Peter Weiss. Yet this provenance says more about the isolation of the intellectual than the paucity of the practice.

Responses

Response

BARBARA CORRELL

I don't expect our discussion to be a disinterested inquiry, and so I'll try to make my own interests clear from the outset.

I'm interested in articulating some discursive spaces of struggle; and in this I have found Victor Burgin and Hal Foster most helpful, not the least for the ways in which their work constitutes for me a kind of revitalization of the project of modernist theory as developed in the German modernism/expressionism debate of the 1930s and in the work of the Frankfurt School.

With the typography/topography of our conference's program in mind, I would point out again (I take it) that in addressing the topic of cultural politics of postmodernity, postmodernity has received the doubt-provoking feature of a diagonally placed divided word set within quotation marks as though to emphasize to us from the outset that though we have a lengthy body of critical and theoretical works addressed to the postmodern, our conference organizers, at least, retain a skeptical or self-reflexive distance; or that if there is a politics of postmodernity, it is accompanied by the question of postmodernity.

I am not so certain that the unfortunate canonization (even if logical/internally logical/following the logic of advanced capitalism and its cultural administrative apparatus) of certain works of modernist culture—the "success" that marks their failure (to scandalize, to disrupt)—marks the end of modernism as cultural political strategy. I'm not sure that we've seen the final containment of what was once their power to activate.

In saying this I certainly do not mean to invoke the mechanistic and relativizing formula of cycles of history or fashion—hemlines rise and fall, what goes round comes round again, docile works become agitational, then again docile—but rather to call attention to the opportunities post-structuralist postmodernism has offered to those, like me, who seek a contestatory and enabling rereading of the past in my own work on the culture of early modernity; and secondly to indicate the opportunity to address some of the issues on the postmodern raised in Habermas' defense of the incomplete project of modernity [or Enlightenment].

My goal, as one who struggles with the challenge of postmodernist theory and culture, as one who wonders honestly whether the project of modernity such as that constructed in the work of Horkheimer and Adorno (in *The Dialectic of Enlightenment*), the modernism debate of German exiles of the 30s, and the work on modernity and communication theory of Jürgen Habermas, awaits completion or has been finished, aborted or rendered obsolete.

Put another way, I want briefly to ponder the role and cultural identity of those European students of the late 1960s— especially those of Adorno, Horkheimer and Habermas themselves—who walked out of their seminars and lectures, urging their professors to critique their own investment in authority structures and to join efforts in a new lesson on cultural politics. Perhaps these students of the struggles in Frankfurt, Berlin, elsewhere, marked the abortive end of the project of modernity—perhaps they constitute an event or text of the postmodern; but they continued to look to these theories to ground and to criticize/reflect upon their ongoing practices.

Horkheimer and Adorno conceive of restless, ceaseless, critical and self-reflexive critical thought—identified as Enlightenment—which can accommodate reflection and thus avoid the retreat from Enlightenment to mythology, although this project remains nostalgically tied to the "redemption of the hopes of the past," to "tendencies toward true humanism," pointing the way toward utopian totality. More importantly, although in their melancholic critique of the culture industry they themselves abandon their own call for critical rigor, their critical theory contains the means by which they might have revised false goals and contributed toward an ongoing contestatory cultural politics.

Similarly, Ernst Bloch in debating Georg Lukacs in the expressionism debate was eager to identify the cultural-political potential of "disruptive and interpolative techniques," of "montage and other devices of discontinuity," "demolition," "of art which strives to exploit the real fissures in surface inter-relations," although he did this with an eye toward an "authentically evolutionary, lucid humanist materialism," invoking again the humanist totality which postmodernism questions.

I do not think these ideas are speciously chosen, that they contrive to produce links that are not apparent and important.

Here I find myself reading Hal Foster with Victor Burgin [just as Burgin reads Mulvey, Rose, Kristeva], thinking about continuity of emancipatory interests in disruptive historical moments. I would point to Foster's call for a theory to understand and situate itself historically, without succumbing to the reduction of reflection theory as Lukacs and, to an unfortunate degree, Jameson and other harsh critics of the postmodernist project.

But much more I would bring in Burgin via Horkheimer and Adorno's critique of Enlightenment. The critical success of Adorno and Horkheimer lies, I believe, in their reading the *Odyssey* as a narrative not so much of a primitive bourgeoisie but rather, more specifically, as the master narrative of instrumental reason and patriarchal relations which first precede, then condition and shape the Enlightenment of Western modernity, and finally follow it. Burgin takes master narrative to the sphere of vision and unmasks the spatial perception, the scopophilic vision/practices of theory which persists in seeing a crisis of the subject, a crisis of order (in which is embedded a call for the reconstruction of order), instead of an exceeding of the patriarchal subject in the rupture of the master narrative in the critical destruction of mastery itself. Such self-reflexive, self-exceeding (not transcending) analyses would pave the way, provide the means by which the contestatory poststructuralist postmodernism would enter (if it has not already entered) the post-patriarchal.

It would seem that Foster and Burgin contribute significantly to a postmodernist politics. Foster comes closer to correcting Habermas' sad misreading of postmodernity in which Habermas shows himself the dutiful heir of Horkheimer and Adorno and their inability to follow their own best rule on Enlightenment, the only way by which the Enlightenment might have, not transcended but exceeded itself—without falling a victim of the dialectic of Enlightenment. Victor Burgin furthers this radical revision by reflecting on the patriarchal privileging of their own method and of enlightenment by which the modern subject is constituted as expression of cultural masculinity which projects Nature and Woman from its own code, from its own geometric and ab-jecting vision.

These new approaches, however, only strive to realize the goal laid out in Horkheimer and Adorno's *Dialectic of Enlightenment*, to create a critique which remains restlessly self- reflexive, self-questioning, or radically reluctant to pause and to resist the temptation to privilege the foundation of its own approach, vocabulary or even object of study. If the postmodernist project can do this—and can continue to do it—with a capacity to elude the forces of cooption, containment and stabilization posed by post-industrial capitalism and its supporting power structures (the fate of modernist art), then it will further the rupturing movement, and we may continue to find in it our collective and disparate efforts, the means for a cultural politics of emancipation.

Response

FREDERICK GARBER

If politics has to do with the confrontation of positions on issues that involve a variety of economies, then postmodernism is eminently political. It is especially so on the issue that Victor Burgin speaks of in terms of the positioning of the subject in space, that Hal Foster points to when he speaks of "integral subjectivity," that sometimes has been called the question of "the unitary self." Though there is clearly some variation among postmodern theorisations on the nature of the self or subject, there are two particular positions which turn up with such regularity that they are frequently presented as quintessentially postmodern, and I shall use these two as my models. The first argues that the self is constituted largely or wholly within language or discourse or representation, that our conviction of the actuality of the self comes from, for example, the grammatical imperative to have a subject to go with a verb and predicate object. The second of these formulations argues that ours is an age of rupture and unstable signs, that the self is therefore necessarily disparate and fragmented, made up of elements that cannot cohere, whatever our nostalgia for an original state of absolute presence and indivisible wholeness. Versions of these and related positions, open and implicit, turn up wherever postmodernism is spoken of at any length.

Yet it seems to me that the issue has not settled into place so easily. Postmodernism has not, in fact, made up its mind on these questions, for their actual status is more varied and complex, and perhaps (in its radical condition) more inherently contradictory, than popular dogma would have it. Some of the major figures associated with postmodern theory seem to be of several minds about these issues; some of the references to the self or subject that we have heard in today's remarks have implications that do not jibe with others that we have heard (compare, for example, the comments of Victor Burgin and Hal Foster); some of the major postmodern writers and artists act as though the comments about the ultimate textuality of the self were made in regard to another body of art than the one we live with now.

Take, for example the remarks with which Hal Foster begins "The Breakup of the Sign in '70s Art." Mr. Foster refers in his introductory paragraph to two basic positions in postmodern art, the one neoconservative, the other poststructuralist, and says that, whatever their differing attitudes toward "historical figuration" and "integral subjectivity," neither can quite escape the fact that "each practice marks the disintegration of both these forms." Further, "each attests to a fetishistic fragmentation of the sign—which poststructuralist theory often valorizes and postmodernist practice often performs."

All of which would seem to make sense of a book like Roland Barthes' late production *Barthes on Barthes*, which the back-cover blurb on the English translation describes, quite properly, as "a kind of autobiography."[1] Of course, we all know what that genre implies: *autos* and *bios*, one's own writing of one's own life, the generic implications as clear as anyone could ask for. There is to be a narrative sequence (open-ended, of course, since it is one's own life that one is writing), the sort of reaching back to beginnings which Sterne parodied at the start of *Tristram Shandy*, and which has always involved the quest for a sustained and coherent narrative which moves out from that point of origin. Barthes, one of our time's master ironists, acceded to the need of autobiography to begin at the beginning; but he does not commence with anything like his own point of origin, whether of the moment of conception, as in Sterne, or the second beginning at birth. Instead, he begins with a point of origin in which we all share, the letter "a"; and the narrative which follows from that beginning is the narrative of the alphabet, pursued as rigorously as one would pursue the sequence of one's life that follows from one's birth. Barthes' "kind of autobiography" is actually a series of comments on various acts and thoughts which are held firmly together by the inflexible tale of the alphabet. The immediate result is a dispersal of the self into a series of fragments which, by virtue of that dispersal, forbids not only a unitary selfhood but any sense of continuity outside a literal (letter-al) one. The ultimate result is a textualization of the self, an identity of self and text which would seem to jibe most neatly with all that we have heard about the postmodern position that the self is constituted largely or wholly within discourse. In fact, what better way to show how this happens than to root one's story of the textualization of the self within the story of the letters whose groupings constitute stories? Barthes, with his usual canniness, sets part of the tone of his parody, and part of the necessary perspective is a prefatory comment: "It must all be considered as if spoken by a character in a novel." Of course, we have to realize that the alphabet does give an order of a kind, a precise and unarguable one; but, considering the point that this is an *auto*biography, the order the alphabet offers is decidedly ironic, for it is so thoroughly impersonal that it can claim no uniqueness, nothing special about the *auto*, since it is shared in by everyone who can read Barthes' text.

So far neatly postmodern, at least as postmodernism is viewed in one of its widely accepted forms. But one also has to consider another late text by Barthes, *Camera Lucida*.[7] Published five years after Barthes' "kind of autobiography" it offers late versions of some of his comments on the photographic image, comments which have much to offer to recent discussions of the index. Barthes' attitude toward questions of presence, of textuality, of authenticity and of continuity takes on a very different look in this late and quite passionate set of musings on photography. Here, for example, are some remarks toward the end of the study which are echoed in their import at every point within it:

> Photography never lies: or rather, it can lie as to the meaning of the thing, being by nature *tendentious*, but never as to its existence. Impotent with regard to general ideas (to fiction), its force is nonetheless superior to everything the human mind can or can have conceived to assure us of reality. . . . Every photograph is a certificate of presence. [p. 87]

Barthes begins the book by describing his feelings when he looked at a photograph of Napoleon's youngest brother Jerome: "I am looking at eyes that looked at the Emperor" (p. 3). He is clearly deeply taken by what photography seems to offer of a kind of unbroken continuity between the object as it existed (whenever it existed), its image in the photograph, and the viewer of that image. The point Barthes makes has been made in various forms from the beginning of comments on photography. The photograph comes into being because light reflected from an object acts on an emulsion to fix an image. As Barthes and so many others have pointed out, the photograph therefore attests to the necessary presence of an independent object. The photograph could not exist without that presence, that having-been-there. To put it in Barthes' words, unlike painting and discourse, "in Photography I can never deny that *the thing has been there*"(p. 76). It seems inevitable for Barthes to argue, as he does on the first page, for a continuum between the object and the image. It seems equally inevitable for him to argue for a peculiar version of "presence" in the photographic image, what Stephen Melville speaks of in his paper as "a certain ineradicable intrusion of the real into art." That which is now and forever absent, Barthes' mother, Napoleon's brother, has in a certain sense stayed on.

Yet Barthes is obviously troubled by this issue, so much so that on the same page on which he argues for the superior reality of the photographic image, he also argues that this "reality" is contingent, that it is, perhaps, "neither image nor reality, a new being, really: a reality one can no longer touch" (p. 87; cf. p. 66). It is clear that Barthes is both uneasy and inconsistent. But it is equally clear that, though his remarks have sometimes been taken as a return to an inappropriate, outdated Realism, he is not so easily taken. He seems mainly to be arguing for a continuum of object and image, a sense of the "that-has-been," a mode of authentication which, he is careful to point out, language can never offer (p. 85).

How can we put into coherent togetherness the shape of *Barthes on Barthes* and the comments of *Camera Lucida*, the argument, on the one hand, for the dispersal of the image and the textualization of self, and the argument, on the other, that the "that-has-been" has been transformed into a new mode of being, continuous with the old and somehow located within the image? Obviously we cannot bring them together lightly or easily, and perhaps we cannot do so at all. Consider, in particular, the way in which the stress on continuity argues for the existence of a profound integrality, the sort of wholeness that any continuum has by definition. It is impossible to square this claim for the integral, for a seamless continuity in which the original object has a sure if unusual place, with the equally intense argument for that disintegration of integral subjectivity, that dismantling of the wholeness of the subject, which so many critics have stated to be characteristically postmodern. Indeed one could bring to this late work of Barthes a variant of the argument Paul de Man brings to the work of Georg Lukács, where de Man accuses Lukács both of arguing for ironic discontinuities between destiny and desire but also of finding, in another context, absolute continuities in a Bergsonian flow of time.[3] Though Barthes denies the idea of the unitary self (with its implicit capacity for transcendence), what he affirms in *Camera Lucida*, by virtue of its stress on a continuum which stems from the original object, goes a good way toward offering a viable substitute for that abandoned wholeness of the subject. *Camera Lucida* begins the way back toward a pure reintegration which would be, at the same time, a refutation of *Barthes on Barthes*. The positions of both books are clearly antithetical, and yet we find both in the late work of a great contemporary theorist.

Similar questions can be asked about some of the writings of Rosalind Krauss who, in her essays on the idea of the index, shows as strong an interest in such matters as Barthes does in his comments on the photographic image. Those essays reveal a considerable concern with an irrefutable trace of the original, its status like that of a footprint or a cast shadow (her examples).[4] The indexical artists to whom Krauss refers argue for a special version of the integral, a sense of radical continuity, but the single show she focuses on in her second essay is by no means unique in its interests and obsessions. Versions of such attitudes can be found in a number of contemporary figures, for, whatever the standard arguments for the fragmentation of the sign, there is clearly an understanding among a variety of artists that the index is, in fact, intensely oxymoronic: not only does it involve a *fragment* of the original object but also a kind of *continuum* between the object and the image. The index, that is, is both part and pointer, remnant and reiteration. (That the index is also a metonym only adds to its complexity and shows how much we have yet to learn about what it is and does.) The status of the index is peculiar and rich with potential, confirming, at the very least, that one can acknowledge the fragmentary and yet acknowledge, at the same time, the concurrent existence of some version of its requisite Other. Such questions occur in the work of Cindy Sherman, who is too often too easily categorized as just another postmodern exponent of the self's fragmentation. Sherman's work is, in one of its aspects, a form of performance art; and in a good deal of performance art (for example, the work of Eleanor Antin) the play of self and its images never quite settles into place, while the matter of the index, with all its difficult decisions about presence and continuity, never quite goes away, never quite settles into the complacency of the contemporary stock response. That issue also haunts the performance poetry of David Antin who, in and out of those performances, worries the question of selfhood in an art form that begins with a spontaneous public performance which is simultaneously taped and then ends on a printed page, the voice always somehow the same yet the conditions of its utterance continually shifting.

No unqualified argument for the absolute textualization of the self can support such practices without considerable qualms and its own big dose of uneasiness. This means that the tensions we see at work in the late writings of Barthes are obviously the property of much more than Barthes himself. Now that postmodernism has settled into general acceptance, no further major breakthroughs likely to appear under its name, we are coming to see that it is actually a complex plurality, promoting a multiplicity of voices whose varied sounds articulate no single, unified stances in, for example, the nature of the subject. We should hardly want it otherwise: given the postmodern antipathy to most sorts of closure, no other stance would be consistent with the way it sees itself.

Notes

1. Trans. Richard Howard (New York: Hill and Wang, 1977).
2. Trans. Richard Howard (New York: Hill and Wang, 1981).
3. See de Man's essay on Lukács in *Blindness and Insight*, 2nd ed. (Minneapolis: University of Minnesota Press, 1983).
4. The essays are in *The Originality of the Avant-Garde and Other Modernist Myths* (Cambridge, Mass, The MIT Press, 1985).

Response

STEPHEN DAVID ROSS

Comments on "Postmodernism": The Future's Future

On this solemn occasion, when we meet to celebrate—few here appear prepared to mourn—the passing of modernity, I should like to consider neither modernity nor its heir, now at the post, but the latter's successor: post-post-modernity, and even post-post-post-post. . . . It is, I know, poor form in such a company to refuse to speak of the dead, though Lyotard suggests that such disregard for form is postmodern. However, perhaps the corpse is not yet still. Perhaps we may question the metanarrative that postmodernism tells of its parent.

How ugly is the child's name! How strange that women should be willing to associate themselves with its phallic post-hum(or)ous imagery. Will the distant progeny continue to be nameless? Will they carry the ancestral name? Is it possible that modernity is still present, not because it is still alive, but because it can have no heir? Yet no future can be guaranteed, certainly not the future's future. No future can guarantee an heir. What, though, would be more terrible than a future without a successor, a future simply the same?—except perhaps one simply different.

Habermas suggests that postmodernity is antimodernity: hostility to the avant-garde. If there is a current avant-garde, let it stand forth and be counted. He does not consider the disturbing possibility that the avant-garde is not dead, but simply used up in the figures that made it possible. Here postmodernity may be neither the successor to modernity nor its repetition, but its shadow, its absent presence, the representation of the representation of what cannot be represented: the visible in the invisible.

I am asking us to think of postmodernity through the figure of time, thereby presenting us with other figures. The primary figure is the fiction that is a future, since it exists only in its representation—is indeed a prominent figure of representation. A future—*one* future—exists for us only in its absence, represented, absent in a deeper negative way than the past—*one* past—whose absence defines representation. Again, representation defines the future for us, while conversely, future and past together define representation. For they are the lived forms of sameness and difference.

The fiction of the future is found wherever it is represented. We may recall the *Terminator*. Among the remarkable features of such a representation are three striking traits: the future is imagined with a past but without a history; it is imagined in the mode of actualized possibility; its terror is that of the same. I again wish to reverse the relation between time and representation. With the figure that is the future lies the figure of both same and different—that is of representation itself. While among the recurrent features of postmodernism is a sense of how the subject and its truth are constituted by power and desire—by a cultural politics and a political culture—that is, by representation, there is no similar attention paid to the constitution of representation by . . . perhaps representation itself, perhaps also by power and desire, but certainly by the future. The politics of representation lies in our images and figures of a future. Or, more accurately perhaps, within the absence of such images.

We might think of modernity arising in the desire for the same within difference: the uniformity of law, the stability of sovereign rule. We might then think of "high" modernity—modern art—as a fear of the same in the shadow of the future. This same is the future's same, and modern artists succeeded modern philosophers, replacing sameness with difference, reason with imagination.

Or perhaps I have this all wrong. I am describing the corpse as if I knew her well in life, though we are far too close for me to know her very well. Desire and power get in the way, since they not only present themselves masked, but impose masks on the clearest of representations. But that is because they are the ways in which contemporary representation defines itself to itself.

The point is not to define modernity, but to suggest that within its futures—and within the future that modernity was to classicism and the Middle Ages—lie the twin specters of sameness and difference: of representation. The dangers are of a future that would be the same, and of a future that would be different. Here the future is both cultural and political. The question of the future is political. It may be what Melville calls ethical.

Post-modernity, in its phallic terminology, seeks to think a future in the mode of representation, thereby largely failing to participate in that future. These are strong words, yet they bear some weight. First, Derrida:

> The future can only be anticipated in the form of an absolute danger. It is that which breaks with constituted normality and can only be proclaimed, *presented*, as a sort of monstrosity.[1]

When Foucault speaks of the "particular, fearsome, and even devilish features" of discourse, he explains not by reference to the future, but to the regulations of the past:

> I am supposing that in every society the production of discourse is at once controlled, selected, organized and redistributed according to a certain number of procedures, whose role is to avert its powers and its dangers, to cope with chance events, to evade its ponderous, awesome materiality.[2]

The future is an absolute abyss. The imagery goes back to the closing images that define Absolute Spirit:

> The goal, which is Absolute Knowledge or Spirit knowing itself as Spirit, finds its pathway in the recollection of spiritual forms as they are in themselves and as they accomplish the organization of their spiritual kingdom.[3]

A future that exists for us only in the mode of recollection is both always the same and an infinite abyss: the negation of the same in difference and the negation of difference in the same. We should hear *différance* in the whispers from the abyss, with the qualification that the tracks are futural more than historical. We cannot *remember* the future.

Melville notes a certain "closure" of postmodernism, represented by a conference such as this. (I will be participating in another on postmodernism at the end of the week.) I suggest a somewhat harsher image: postmodernism is already canonical, already insistently repetitive. It demands its own successor. Images of repetition recur throughout. Foster speaks of the fragmentation of signs that marks the ruptures of modernism—a fragmentation in which signs repeat themselves endlessly. Images such as fetishization, commodification, reification, and exchange equivalencies simultaneously repeat both the mass marketing of capitalist production and themselves. Burgin emphasizes the "cone of vision" that defines modern representational space; implicit in such a picture is the homogeneity that typically defines extension: any location is like any other.

Some of his lines are worth noting:

> No space of representation with a subject, and no subject with a space it is not. (24)

> [Space] has a history, it is a product of representations. (17)

Foucault said in an interview about the second and third parts of the *History of Sexuality*, years after suggesting in *The Order of Things* that the modern subject was constituted by representation, that the common theme throughout all his works was the constitution of the subject. The subject here is both a constant and variable, a sameness in difference, but also a difference in sameness. To say this is to say not merely that the subject is constituted by representation, but that representation is constituted by the subject and its major representatives: subjectivity, desire, power, and truth. The doubling of both subject and representation in relation to power and desire is fundamental. The autonomous subject is subjected to desire; the representative sign is an emissary of power.

Perhaps the most wonderful of Burgin's references is the bloody passage from Klaus Theweleit:

> I'll be in a state where everything is the same inextricably mixed together. (26)

This image of the same mixed all together—almost pre-Socratic—can be matched only by an equally hyperbolic image of the different as *always* different—almost Heraclitean. We return—what else?—to the same and different that constitute the future and the future's futures. Like good Hegelians, we must not attempt to imagine the future, not only because our imaginations are always too late, but because any imagined future can only be a representation of its past.

Whether, then, we may deliver ourselves from modernity into postmodernity is a difficult question, not because modernity is itself the end, or because the powers that have captured it are beyond resistance. The name "postmodernity" is simultaneously apt and forbidding: apt because whatever future it marks, and its own future, offers the threat of simply more of the same to those who are terrified by sameness, and the threat of difference to those who crave the same. The picture of the world may be given up, but only through another representation, not only because the world exists only as represented, but because representation exists only as mimetic. In this sense, to say, as Lyotard suggests in his account of postmodernism, that the sublime is found everywhere, or as Melville claims, that the sublime "disrupts all frames" is to return to the same from within difference, to return to the place from which we sought to flee.

All of this—again, the same—is political, not merely because it has political consequences or because representation is influenced by power. The question of the future is political. And it is a question I have been suggesting is masked within the representations that define postmodernism. Melville suggests that the rhetoric of postmodernism "licenses—and stakes—at once everything and nothing." (4) If this is criticism—and it must be the basis of his ethical alternative— we must add to it the point that from a future standpoint everything and nothing is always at stake, along with sameness and difference. We appear here to return to Derrida's absolute monstrosity and Foucault's perilousness of discourse. Yet there is a difference amidst the similarity: that the inexhaustible finiteness that is at stake in the future is simply its finiteness and the finiteness of praxis. The twin reefs of the future, sameness and difference, appear most prominently in the form of rules; and there is no practice that does not both conform to rule and deviate from rule, no practice that is not hermeneutic: mediative and disruptive.

I will conclude with a somewhat tangential reference, motivated by the theme of power in relation to the future. A recurrent motif in much postmodern discourse is a certain hostility to technology, even to science. In part, this hostility derives from a sense of the abuses of capitalism. In further part, it derives from a recognition that science and technology are both blind to their own representational nature. In still further part, it derives from the fear that representation—especially including art—is in danger of being captured by technology. What must be added, on the other side, is that science and technology each belong to the future in a way that far transcends any prospects in current postmodernism. Or perhaps I should have said that the future belongs to them. That such a prospect is disturbing is not merely a consequence of the awful powers of science and technology, but is inherent in the nature of our relationship to the future.

There are two fundamental ways in which we may deny the future. One is by denying the past, and here science and technology in their modern forms face the future backwards. The other is by too much talk, especially about power, without a strong enough sense of what matters and what does not. Here technology is the heart of postmodernism, both because any imaginable future will be technological and because technology is the material form of practical power. In this sense, postmodernism is frequently a voice crying out to a future it cannot bear to imagine.

Notes

1. Jacques Derrida, *On Grammatology*, trans. G. Spivak (Baltimore: Johns Hopkins University Press, 1974) 5.
2. Michel Foucault, "The Discourse on Language" (translation of "L'ordre du discours"), appendix to *The Archaeology of Knowledge*, trans. R. Swyer (New York: Pantheon, 1972) 216.
3. G. W. F. Hegel, *The Phenomenology of Mind*, trans. J. B. Baillie (London: Allen & Unwin, 1931) 808.

Response

MAUREEN TURIM

One of the things that strikes me about postmodernism is how various this term is in its application in different fields. Postmodernism has been used by artists, musicians, architects somewhat differently than postmodernism as it's been used by theorists. This difference points to an issue that can be addressed theoretically, the gaps that exist between different praxes. For many artists, postmodernism has been a pragmatic means of stylistic and conceptual differentiation from a tradition of form and theory that they otherwise might have simply inherited. It is a way to succeed or supercede the legacy of modernism. It is sometimes a rejection of much of what modernism represented and actualized, sometimes a reaction to the taming and cooptation of modernism, sometimes simply an acknowledgement that times have changed and there is something different to be made that has its own logic and imperative. In all instances, a response to mass culture and popular forms is apparent in postmodernism as style.

For theorists, and this includes those artists steeped in theory, these shifts are symptomatic of desires and social conditions that are engaged conceptually. One of the emblems of such engagement with postmodernism is Jean-François Lyotard's *La Condition Postmoderne*, especially in its English translation that begins with Fredric Jameson's forward, following from Jameson's own earlier writing on postmodernism. Emblematic, for here in one volume post-structural French thought confronts the Frankfurt school and is in turn confronted by the recent Marxist reassessment of Frankfurt school approaches to culture. Lyotard says that postmodernism imposes a reexamination of the thought of the Enlightenment. He means to overcome the limits that he sees in the Frankfurt school, with due respect, perhaps to Benjamin, but certainly Adorno remains the devil. A particular focus is on the critique of the historical linearity of development, on the need to look at culture as analogous to the stages of history, and the stages of capitalism in particular. At the same time, it is not simply a dismissal of reflection theory, but a reexamination of what it might mean to see culture in context. The assumed analogy, the apriori analogy is called into question. The role in the formation of culture of two things that Marxism has had a problem addressing, language and technology, becomes key. For Lyotard, unlike Jameson, the split between high modernism and postmodernism in culture is not one of a periodic history corresponding to stages in the development of capital. It is a blurred edge, an uneven development. One of the most disturbing and intriguing aspects of postmodern theory is that in its view events, artifacts and responses won't simply fit onto the time-line of art history mapped against social and economic history; and yet, unlike formalism, it wants to account for contexts. Theories of reflection are tempered with a notion of heterogeneity and multiple determination, using the findings of textual analysis and theories of reading and spectatorship.

While in artistic practice postmodernism implies a kind of antimodernism, in the theoretical view this is not necessarily the case. Postmodern theory is more conscious of itself as an extension of modernism, a point that was brought out in more than one of the papers and responses here. It has more at stake in deconstructing periodization, even that implied by its own "name." The avant-gardes of modernist art usually retain their value in postmodern theory, even as they are being recontextualized as movements of a past whose conditions are no longer those facing the artist today. Still, Lyotard's definition of postmodernism as the unrepresentable in representation, a definition which reformulates what representation might mean in reference to psychoanalysis, hasn't come up here in that form. Yet in different ways two of the papers do, I think, play with this notion of the postmodern.

Constance Penley's look at the same narrative addressed in different forms, by an avant-garde work and a work characteristic of commercial mass culture, tells us of the desire that circulates in both forms. It is in a sense postmodern to bring these works into juxtaposition despite their differences in form, audience, and period of production. Penley resists evaluation, introducing it in her final paragraphs, as she points out differences, then steps back and refuses the dichotomy, and the hierarchy of interest it implies. If I raise a question about this aspect of a postmodernist handling of commercial and marginal cultural productions, it is not because I do not respect the theoretical motivations of the equalization of attention. It is that I am worried that in this formulation, the theorization of desire and the unrepresentable is flattened. The contestatory and innovative can no longer be set apart from those works which reproduce the forms and mythologies of the past. *The Terminator* strikes me as self-consciously, stylistically and thematically striving to appear postmodern, fashionable, up-to-date, but to be mired in a representation that all too clearly presents its messages, mundane and ideologically pernicious messages that we have seen and heard in a hundred popular tales of the hero and heroine, the family, who defeat the forces of evil, here cast as the future of technology. Females are recruited as earth mothers, nurturers, while the man can be father and son, past and present hero at once. I think if postmodern attention to audience and desire is to have any import, the modes and functions of a given representation must still receive critical attention, even if that induces certain evaluative dichotomies. While it is valuable to analyze the emergence of an aspect of critical dystopia alongside this mythological regurgitation, I feel we simultaneously need a concept of otherness in language, in art, to speak of more inspired works that take on a truly postmodern project, that are theoretically informed.

"Psychical realism" in Victor Burgin's formulation appears to be a wish for an artistic and theoretical practice that moves beyond Euclidian models to image a space of changing geometries. What is attractive here is the focus on the unconscious and desire in connection with an investigation of perceptual assumptions and ideological reinforcement, and the essay draws together many strands of contemporary thought on the picture plane, subject positioning and the construction of the psyche. Disturbing is an undercurrent of attack on feminist criticism that culminates in, "It is thanks to such positivism, for example, that certain critics can pay lip service to psychoanalytic theory while speaking of scopophilia as if there were nothing more to say about it than that it is a morally reprehensible form of behavior of men." Does one detect a defensive posture here by a subject who remains male-identified? To circumscribe the feminist critiques of representation as positivist is precisely to evacuate the history of representation that one claims to be describing and overcoming. The danger is again repetition, repetition of images which despite their changing geometries reproduce outmoded sexual roles for both image-object and viewer-subject. That postmodernism take on a complex "mutation of space in which the very dichotomy of man/woman as an opposition between two rival entities may be understood as belonging to metaphysics" (Burgin's citation from Kristeva), should not mean that images which fix that very metaphysics be allowed to pass for the circulation of desire or any kind of new space.

To return to Lyotard, let's consider a statement he makes about the role that photography and cinematography have within postmodern theory: they cannot reproduce painting and literature, for once they do, they fall into a mass conformism of communication. I think it is incumbent upon us to theorize how all the arts, photography and cinematography perhaps exemplary in this regard, need detach themselves from reproduction of the past in a manner that is not simply the dismissal of representation, of the icon, that was presented in high modernism (although I, at least, do not mean to turn abstract high modernism into the assumed negative, but rather to see its potential for opening other spaces) but rather a reworking of representation, so that it address repetition and fixing as institutional imperatives. Desire cannot be channelled in postmodern art in the same old ways.

Afterword

Afterword

MICHAEL WALSH

Sometimes I Feel Like an Otherless Child

Late in the afternoon of "The Cultural Politics of 'Postmodernism,'" moderator John Tagg remarked that each and every term in the title of the symposium had come under critical fire, including article and particle, "the" and "of." Oddly unscathed, however, were the diacritical marks which might in the first place have been expected to provoke comment. Let me rectify this oversight, even if its omission on the day derived from its obviousness as a sally. To place "postmodernism" in scare-quotes is to indicate a healthy skepticism about the intellectual or historical status of the term; however, beyond serving as an economical method of posing the now-familiar question, "What can postmodernism mean?", the quotes also lead discussion away from the putative substance of the term and toward its disruptive effects and activations. The experience of the day suggested that these might now be assessed in terms of their inertia; contributions to an already mature discussion might best be evaluated insofar as they are able to escape from the compulsion to repeat certain overly-familiar strategies and imperatives.

This criterion is not entirely fair, yet it is forced upon us by a debate which seems as finally elusive as it is immediately repetitious. Perhaps postmodernism is itself postmodern; vexing, contradictory, dissimulating rather than simulating, undecided if not actually undecidable. For some commentators (the Jameson school of Marxists, represented at the symposium by Hal Foster) postmodernism is nothing less than epochal;

it is the third great cultural transformation within the history of capitalism, corresponding to the third of the industrial revolutions detailed by Ernest Mandel in *Late Capitalism*. For others (Derrideans and de Manians, represented at the symposium by Stephen Melville) the traditional understanding of politics, position, and period is deeply epistemologically suspect; what is now considered postmodern can always-already be found in Modernism, in Romanticism, in the Enlightenment. Others yet pursue strategies less indebted to either Derrida or Jameson; at Binghamton, Victor Burgin and Constance Penley dealt rather more obliquely and perhaps more productively with the question of postmodernism, converging on the issue of sexual difference.

As I have said, my criteria are not entirely fair, stressing in the case of Stephen Melville less his intellectual brilliance and more his allegiance to de Manian deconstruction. For Melville, the postmodern is corrosive of positions as such, deconstructive of the "terms and structures through which (one) recognizes or acknowledges a position as political." Delicate in his dealing with Kant's third *Critique* and Heidegger's essay on "The Age of the World Picture," Melville proved capable of discovering genuine contradictions in our notion of representation, which he described as unable either to completely become itself or to completely efface itself. He also began a promising inquiry into the aesthetics of photography, which he considered the postmodern art par excellence, insofar as it "sticks us with our worldliness and delivers us from what we have learned to call 'aestheticism' and 'formalism.' "

Rather less satisfying were the larger shapes of his argument. Despite sporadic suggestions that he sought actively to reimagine the prevailing conception of politics, he seemed quite straightforwardly intent on attacking the Marxism of Fredric Jameson. Such at least was the apparent subtext of a discussion in which a "politically programmatic" appropriation of postmodernism was perceived to endanger a "theory of writing," while "the eternal return of the same" was imagined to oblige a revision of our notions of time and history. In a criticism of "the hope that through theory we will gain or ground a politics," Melville revealed the thoroughgoing idealism of his conception of the activity of those to his left. While Jameson's recent work is clearly vulnerable to the charge with which Derrida once twitted Lacan, that of a "massive recourse to Hegel," it is far from clear why American Derrideans, themselves so vulnerable to charges of political indifference, see their most appropriate responses as the retreat into a quite unreconstructed deconstruction.

One possibility is that they see this "retreat" more as a reassertion.

In his 1983 lectures on Paul de Man, Derrida continues to advise us that there is no politics without text; should we wonder who exactly remains unapprised of this, he includes a nuanced criticism of those for whom "deconstruction is the specular image of the society of the spectacle." The citation is from John Brenkman, but this is also of course the position of Fredric Jameson and Hal Foster. At Binghamton, the latter picked up where his essay "(Post)Modern Polemics" left off, with the proposition that neoconservative postmodernism (Julian Schnabel) and poststructuralist postmodernism (Laurie Anderson) participate equally in a "fetishistic fragmentation of the sign" and a "spectacular reification" which is "fundamental to the logic of capital." Far from eroding the fixities of politics and position, poststructuralism in philosophy is indexical of the culture of multinational capital.

Discussing the Barthes of *S/Z* and the Derrida of "Structure, Sign, and Play," Foster linked and valorized Jameson and Baudrillard (who had been sharply contrasted by Melville), saying that both perceive capital as the ultimate agent of the modernist abstraction of the referent and the postmodernist abstraction of the signified. On this basis, he proceeded to an assessment of 70's art theory, in the principal persons of Rosalind Krauss, Craig Owens, and Benjamin Buchloh. One might have been forgiven for wondering whether any significant theory of 70's art was devised by someone not closely associated with *Artforum* and *October*, but the burden of Foster's argument was that while these critics actually narrated the breakup of the sign, their historical circumstances prevented them from recognizing capital as the motive force in that dissipation.

As in the case of Melville, Foster's real strength lay in his specific analyses of texts obviously important to him, and his thinking proved nimbly dialectical. His conclusions, however, seemed somewhat contradictory. On the one hand, he offered a deeply-felt jeremiad against the cynical conventionalism of much contemporary art; on the other, his call for artists to join with socially excluded groups and become "collective producers" seemed the merest of political wish- fulfillments. If, by his own earlier logic, capital was so easily able to subsume Krauss, Owens, and Buchloh, this final imperative, predicated on an "effort of will," seemed surprisingly naive.

Melville had begun by calling himself a "reactionary;" Foster concluded by calling himself a "utopian." It was too easy to agree with both of them, too easy to see their efforts to outflank and contain each other as the mutual necessity of habits of thought contained within an airless if not exactly vicious circle. Given the intellectual stature of the two, it was also necessary to wonder whether these were the only conceivable options.

The first hint of an alternative was provided by Constance Penley, whose discussion of *The Terminator* could be seen as the reinscription under the postmodern rubric of an object (the somewhat sophisticated Hollywood film) and a method (feminist psychoanalysis) familiar from other, earlier dispensations of criticism. The strengths of Penley's presentation lay in her good humor and her attention to the film's particular textures, especially a careful delineation of mise-en-scene in terms of "tech noir." Also intriguing was the discovery of the Freudian primal scene as the basis of the appeal of the time-travel scenario, though one might have wished for a more critical deployment of this most pivotal concept in the most classical narrative of psychoanalysis. Even so, this argument provided the impetus for a wide- ranging discussion of sexual difference in the science-fiction film, concluding with an assessment of Chris Marker's *La Jetée.* According to Penley, we might consider *The Terminator* a remake of *La Jetée* were it not that the earlier film's manipulation of time-loop paradoxes renders it actually unrepeatable—an argument which went a good distance toward developing the complexities of psychic time which had been intimated by the mention of the primal scene.

It was left to Victor Burgin to indicate the full extent to which the discussion of postmodernism could escape from the circle of received ideas. "Geometry and Abjection" was a critical history of the "cone of vision" model of space, representation, and ideology. Finding the origin of the model in Euclidean geometry, and considering the Renaissance as the moment at which the cone of vision was intersected by the picture plane, Burgin elaborated on the theoretical effects of an argument summarized thus by Barthes: "there will always be representation for so long as a subject (author, reader, spectator, or voyeur) casts his gaze towards a horizon, on which he cuts out the base of a triangle, his eye (or his mind) forming the apex." Burgin enlarged methodically and convincingly on the thesis that the cone of vision is equally inappropriate to psychoanalytic theory and to the postmodern apprehension of space, within which both Euclidean and Renaissance geometries have been eclipsed by what Paul Virilio calls a "space of time."

Burgin too had canonical 70's texts to read, Laura Mulvey's "Visual Pleasure and Narrative Cinema" and Jacqueline Rose's "The Imaginary." His determination to read them together was designed to support his contention that while their deployment of the cone of vision model had the virtue of posing the question of the place of the subject in the space of representation, it did little to challenge the understanding of the subject/object dichotomy as a relation of inside and outside. While a more radical psychoanalytic theory sees the splitting of the subject as obviating the subject/object dichotomy, 70's theory tended to gravitate back toward the punctual ego which it was supposed to subvert.

Taking his cue from Julia Kristeva's *Powers of Horror*, Burgin found the origin of geometry in abjection, "the means by which the subject is first impelled towards the possibility of constituting itself as such, in an act of revulsion." Yet the sense in which abjection actually lies beyond the rhetoric of subject and object is debatable. A first doubt arises when abjection is described as previous in the history of the subject to its constitution as such; a theory quite sceptical of prevailing notions of space and time might work harder to problematize the chronologies which underpin the Freudian narrative. If psychical reality is in fact capable of superimposing subject and object, then surely it also sustains prolepses and metalepses which complicate the assumption that abjection is prior to subject and object. A similar kind of question might be asked about the objects of abjection, although in Kristeva this is the feminist point of the concept: the first object of abjection is the pre-Oedipal mother, giving rise to that "peripheral ambivalence of the position allocated to woman which has led to that familiar division in which women are either saintly or demonic. . . ."

Such conclusions were peculiarly intriguing insofar as the half-hidden agenda of Burgin's paper was the feminist criticism of certain of his own images of women, such as the peepshow nude in his Berlin series, his underclothed version of Manet's "Olympia," and even his woman worker in the recent "Office at Night" series. The charge against Burgin is not one of simple sexism but one of remaining fascinated by images which he claims to criticize; at the same time, he can be seen as a courageous rarity among male artists in his refusal to opt for the safety of simply excluding such issues from his work. Without adjudicating this debate, however, one might still question the extent to which the end of the subject/object dichotomy is the end of the objectification of women; indeed, Burgin's paper could be read, slightly against the grain, as an account of the endurance of that dichotomy even when its ideological status has been exposed. Again then, one might discriminate between the general principle of an argument and the specific ends to which it worked. Burgin afforded psychoanalysis its proper status as a genuine logic, following through on his premises with clear-eyed determination.

Whether the rhetoric of subject and object had been surpassed and whether male objectification of women has been rendered less pressing as an issue remained open questions.

In a plenary session, Frederick Garber pursued the sense in which postmodern criticism has no stable concept of subjectivity, teasing out the contradictions in two late texts of Barthes, *Camera Lucida* and *Barthes on Barthes.* While William Spanos launched a political critique of Stephen Melville, and Steven David Ross attacked postmodernism in the name of a future which he claimed it cannot imagine, Barbara Correll argued for a postmodernism of resistance, a "contestatory and enabling reading of early modernity." The day's final speaker was Maureen Turim, who inspired some of the commentary above by remarking on the curious displacement of ahistorical deconstruction by historicist postmodernism. In the concluding discussion, Hal Foster suggested the title of this review by asking "What is the other of postmodernism?" If it has no self, it has no other.

1997